MY JOURNEY WITH DEERFOOT

A Path of Discovery and Learning within the Flintlock Rifle Tradition

by

John W. Hayes

Phil 4:13 - I can do all things through Christ who strengthens me.

ISBN 978-0-9793399-4-3 (paperback)
ISBN 978-0-9793399-5-0 (e-book)

Copyright © 2023 by John W. Hayes

All rights reserved. No part of this publication may be reproduced, distributed or transmitted in any form or by any means, including photocopying, recording or other electronic or mechanical methods without the prior written permission of the publisher. For permission requests, solicit the publisher via the address below.

Publisher:
Hunting Through History
38110 County Road 469
Cohasset, MN 55721
www.huntingthroughhistory.com

Printed in the United States of America

Front cover - The hoof print of a deer made from German silver inlaid into the cheek rest of the rifle, which gave the rifle its name.
Back cover - Author firing Deerfoot while on the trail in the woods of Minnesota.
All photos are attributed to Author, unless otherwise marked.

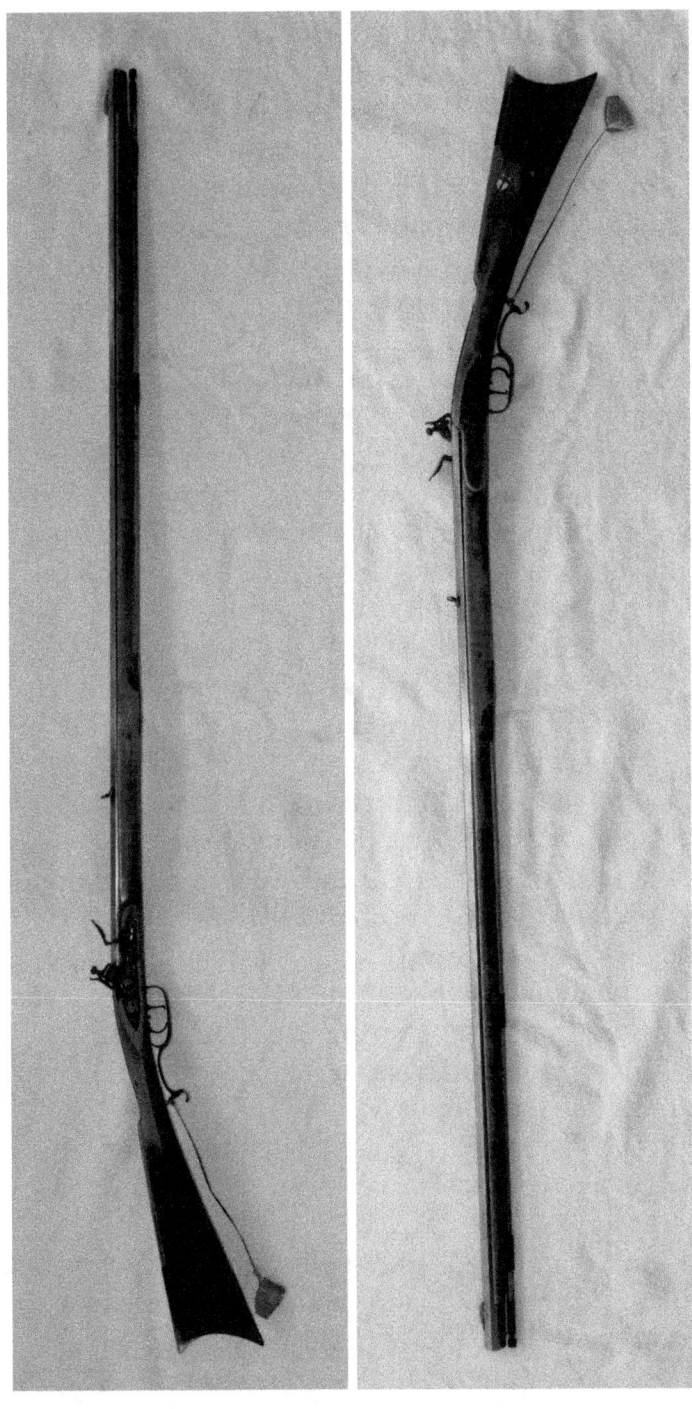

Deerfoot: Top- lockside and Bottom-opposite side. Stocked in plain maple sporting a straight 13/16" Rice barrel, forty-one inches in length and bored in .45 caliber with 7 round-bottomed rifling. Double-set Davis triggers, small Siler flintlock. A frizzen cover is tied to the rear of the trigger guard's open scroll.

Acknowledgements

Special thanks to my wife Connie Hayes whose contributions are too numerous to list. She kept the home fires burning and continues to support me in my pursuit of historical lifeways. She always makes time for me to relate my adventures whether two hours, two days, or two weeks. I especially love it when she can join me in those endeavors.

To my daughter, Johannah Hayes, thank you for helping with the original manuscript and fresh ideas for my approach to composition. Thanks to: Joshua Shepherd, Mark Roster, Cheri Roster and Mark Sage for your scrutiny.

Thank you to the artisans who generously gave me of their time, namely: Simeon England, Mike Miller, Eugene Shadley, Keith Johnson, Wallace Gusler, Bill Carpenter and Bob Odegard.

I also need to acknowledge H. David Wright, Jim Chambers, Mel Hankala, and Clay Smith who were willing to spend time with me and answer *all* my questions, whether in person or by phone. To Bill Scurlock and Jason Gatliff, past and present senior editors of **Muzzleloader Magazine**, thank you for providing me with a platform to share my experiences. Also, thanks to the folks at **Muzzle Blasts** for publishing my manuscripts.

Thank you to the brigade, Upper Mississippi Alliance of Adventurers, including Larry Spisak. Also, to Gerry Barker and Mark A. Baker, thanks for sharing time in the many camps, as well as, in the woods, and on the waters. Thanks to all the other folks like Paul Jones, Roger Cook, "Crazy Jake," and Duane "Bish" Bischoff, who generously shared their time, knowledge, and practical-experience, with me in my journey.

Above all, I thank Jesus Christ who has changed my life, and guided me through the mountain top experiences and struggles in the valleys. I have never had to walk alone!

Forward

I have known John Hayes for a very long time. We have hunted together, traveled many miles to many different historical events, visited museums, camped together and walked the same path of historical discovery in muzzleloading. One thing is for sure; John's pursuit of history is very similar to his tracking of game - he gets on the trail and relentlessly stays on it till he finds what he is looking for!

John has both a very scientific mind and a love of the woods, and both of these interests come into play in his exploration of our frontier history.

This book is about John's metamorphosis from modern-day muzzleloading into a deper understanding of our frontier history and those frontiersmen who lived in a time of unprecedented freedom to roam and discover the land that we live upon today - one that is covered with tar and cement, strip malls and highways, and over-littered with social media.

John has skillfully related in his book how a simple inanimate object (his rifle named Deerfoot) became a vehicle of discovery in his quest to connect with our past. Further, he has enhanced it with interesting and educational stories that both the experienced muzzleloading enthusiast and those new to the experience with benefit from.

-Mark Steven Sage, Author and Public Presenter-

Table of Contents

Chapter 1	The Spark	p. 1
Chapter 2	The Package	p. 21
Chapter 3	The Tipi Diversion	p. 45
Chapter 4	The Conversion Begins	p. 55
Chapter 5	Three Diversions or rather Stepping Stones	p. 70
Chapter 6	Molded by Tradition	p. 79
Chapter 7	My Expanding Efforts with Flintlocks	p. 85
Chapter 8	Hard Won Lessons	p. 93
Chapter 9	Focussing on the Fowler	p. 98
Chapter 10	A Breath of Fresh Air	p. 111
Chapter 11	The Next Horizon	p. 121
Chapter 12	Looking Backward, Looking Forward	p. 135
Chapter 13	The First Time to Go-it Alone	p. 151
Chapter 14	Revelations from an Old Barrel	p. 161
Chapter 15	The Legacy Continues	p. 171
Chapter 16	The Commodity of Skill, the Value of Experience	p. 181
Chapter 17	The Tennessee Rifle	p. 191
End Notes		p. 203

Chapter 1
The Spark

One spring, not so long ago, I sat in the tavern room of my basement, looking across the cobbled brick floor at a simple rifle and thought about its journey with me which really became the "road less travelled." I have to admit, that because of that "road," I am truly enriched and blessed. As cliché as it sounds, that really has made all the difference. I look on the rifle now as an old friend, a sort of mentor that encouraged me to face a myriad of challenges which were just waiting to be posed and begging to be engaged.

The humble muzzleloader stood leaning against the wall, in the company of coats, hunting frocks, felt hats and shooting bags with powder horns; hanging from a line of shaker pegs. I thought about the rifle's long history with my family, including my dogs, and me. The modest .45 caliber, Tennessee flintlock rifle sports a straight 41" octagon barrel, a plain, non-figured maple stock and iron hardware. Lastly, inlaid into the cheek rest, in German silver, is the small hoof-print of a deer, hence the name **Deerfoot.**

That journey was prefaced, like most, with a goal in mind; to own a longrifle. My romantic notions had been spurred on by actor, Fess Parker, in his roles as TV's Daniel Boone and the several movies in Walt Disney's franchise of Davey Crockett. These two characters, brought to life by Fess Parker's Hollywood portrayal, each sported a long muzzleloading firearm. It was a "package deal." Neither character, would be considered a complete frontiersmen nor ready for the wilderness without that long gun in his hand and powder horn with pouch at his side. Therefore, as a young lad, I too sought to be accoutred with a similar long gun and various pouches.

My Journey with Deerfoot

Another aspect of this journey involves my education as a youth, in the schools of Northern Virginia; Fairfax County to be exact. There I learned that I lived in an area steeped in Colonial History and traditions. A thirty-minute drive might bring me to any number of places such as: George Washington's Mount Vernon, Woodlawn, or Washington's grist mill on Turkey Creek. Not far from that sits Belvoir of the Fairfax family, friends of Washington. Further to the south lie numerous plantation houses and sites of the eighteenth century.

Moreover, my friends and I found the occasional round ball or American Civil War bullet while spending our time along the creeks and runs nearby. The roundball and conical projectiles we discovered were constant reminders of the use and prevalence of muzzleloading guns in our past, which had actually been used historically right in our own stomping-grounds.

This area left me with a definite bias towards colonial lifestyle and a lifelong bond with Virginia as both a colony and state.

My parents played a part in this as well, because they recognized my love of all things from the colonial frontier to the cowboy era. My birthday gifts, for instance, at the age of nine, consisted of a new fringed leather jacket and a lever-action pop-gun that actually shot wine-bottle corks. In the shipping box which held the pop-gun; however, was the real ticket to the start of my journey. In that box, I found a one-page list of toy "longrifles" and pistols from Frontier Arms. There were several "carbines" representing the civil war which were interesting, but not really my cup of tea.

What really caught my eye was the representation of a much earlier, much longer-barreled "Colonial Rifle." I

The Spark

made sure to safely store that catalog or rather flyer, but not before I had put a check mark by that long gun. On occasion, I would peruse that flyer and consider owning that quintessential emblem of the frontier man. About a year later I was done waiting. I bought the cap-gun interpretation of a "Colonial" longrifle.

The cost was about $11.00 and with shipping added an extra $2.95 or so, the total came to around $14.00. I paid for it with money from my paper-route. Pursuant to the terms of order-fulfillment in the catalog, the order would take four to six weeks for delivery, which to a ten-year old, seemed like an eternity. All that was left to do was wait and try not to think about it.

When the "colonial era longrifle," finally arrived in mid November, I tore into the box and removed the long awaited prize. At the time I did not know anything about style. The barrel was not attached with pins, rather it was attached with bands, like a musket. It had an actual ramrod of steel - no doubt for durability - instead of a wooden ramrod. There were no sights to speak of, the butt plate was merely brass colored paint and the patchbox was nothing more than a decal. Lastly, the stock was cut from a pine board. None of that mattered, however to my ten-year old eyes and mind-set.

Oh my goodness! I finally had something I could weild and refer to as a longrifle, because that is what the catalog called it. Its arrival was also ushered in with an early snowfall which blanketed the area with about two inches of wet snow; the sort of weather Virginia drivers dread and even curse.

In my youthful, romantic, exuberance, the snow blanketing the landscape created the perfect autumn ambience. It was the kind of weather intrepid frontiersmen endured when hunting and tending traps. Additionally, I felt infinitely connected to Daniel Boone and his era, because, I was also reading a book about Daniel Boone authored by William O. Steele.[1]

Every time I traipsed into the woods of our vacant-lot wearing my fringed leather jacket, I had the longrifle in my hand and I was ready for my own wilderness trek. My adolescent's goal had been achieved. I had a longrifle and felt like a complete frontiersman.

The Steady Build-Up

Fast forward a few years and with the release of **Jeremiah Johnson**, starring Robert Redford, the fervor to recreate the independent man of the mountains was invading the minds of many would-be outdoorsmen. This was also followed by the Bicentennial celebrations which made constant reference to the year 1776 when the flintlock was king. The outdoor catalogs were quick to seize on the opportunity to participate in the market and offered an array of muzzleloading rifles and pistols.

Given the fervor and constant reminders, I never forgot the feeling of being accompanied by that toy longrifle on my adventures. As I matured, however I wondered what it would take to obtain an actual working, black powder longrifle.

During my Freshman year in high school, I considered the possibility many times of buying such a rifle. Logic, however, intervened in my thoughts to persuade me otherwise. My ruminations went something like: *I already had several rifles, modern ones that worked just fine. Why did I need that gun, with all the extra stuff that goes with it? Couldn't I just put a brass butt-plate or brass fore-end*

The Spark

on the stock of a modern rifle, and have that suffice? That manner of thinking usually sucked the romance from my head and moved me to ignore the offerings for muzzleloaders in the outdoor catalogs, never the less, those images provoked my thoughts and refused to be dampened by logic. Romance continued to fuel a desire that remained hot within me, like a glowing coal, just under the surface of the ash.

During the summer of 1977, I purchased a modern 30-06 rifle while working with my Uncle George on the family farm, near Kindred, North Dakota. Shortly after the purchase, my Uncle George, my brother Bob and I headed to the farm of Sam Vangsness, to have a day of shooting along with Sam's sons, Curty and Sinster.

I had shot my new rifle about ten times that morning when Curty and Sinster brought out their new acquisition in the form of an original .58 caliber Zouave military musket. As if to spur on the "frontiersman" hidden within me, I watched as each of them shot it. I was spellbound. I just had to have a try for myself.

The brothers were more than happy to accommodate my request. I studied their process of loading powder, conical bullet, and capping the nipple before handing it to me.

I aimed at a stick in the mud of the Sheyenne River and hit it causing it to cast over, but not breaking it. Well, that was all it took for me. The rest of that day, I ended up shooting that musket more than I did my new modern rifle. Everyone now made a game out of shooting at the triangle formed by the clipped stick, calling their shot and then trying their skill. I also called my shots, but with the Zouave, and it really did not matter whether I hit my target, if I came close. I believe I was hooked that very day, I just did not know it at

My Journey with Deerfoot

the time.

Perhaps, one day, I too might own such a gun, but as before, daydreams would have to take a back-seat to reality and logic. Thank you Curty & Sinster for fanning that glowing ember.

From my youth I had been taught to conserve my money and spend only when I needed to. I had just purchased a brand new deer rifle, so the thought of buying another gun was out of the question. Instead, I saved my money for; college, a vehicle, gas and maintenance, the occasional hunting and fishing trip, oh yes, and moccasin boots. As I said, "necessities."

My first reasonable opportunity to purchase a true working black powder rifle would not make Deerfoot a reality, rather Deerfoot would actually be my second black powder rifle.

As with many things in life, my first longrifle would not just happen all at once. I would have to inch-my-way to that prize over a number of years. In retrospect it seems that I was being tested. If I really wanted a muzzleloader that would emulate the era of Boone, Lewis & Clark and Crockett, I would have to work for it.

In the summer of 1981, I was introduced to a local black powder muzzleloading club at the home of Herman Kossow, near LaPrairie Minnesota. As host, Herman used the shooting range in his back yard for the monthly shoots. There were a number of members in attendance on each of these two club shoots.

On the first visit, I recall throwing my tomahawk against several competitors and picking up some valuable tips, as well as talking to Herman about a deer hide that he had stretched and was ready to tan. I told him about my

The Spark

tanning background, having done several dozen hides, and we continued to chat for some time. He made me feel very welcome that day.

The following month on my second visit, I arrived in time to actually do some shooting. I recall Dot Kossow loading her .36 caliber T/C Cherokee caplock rifle and then handing it to me. This she did as long as I wanted to shoot it, which was at least fifteen times. I even competed in a quarter shoot, but did not win.

While there, a tall gent by the name of Roger Cook presented me with his long barreled flintlock rifle, which I shot and barely hit the target. I was not used to the flash at the pan which jarred my concentration. Somehow, I still kept my wits enough to maintain a steady hold. I made some remark about the flash and everyone watching me chuckled about my first experience with a flintlock rifle. Thank you, Roger Cook, for "priming the pan."

I ended up visiting Roger, his wife Marge and his two boys at their home on Bass Lake. I watched as he prepared to inlet a flintlock on a stock and thought to myself, *It is going to take quite a while to finish that gun, I doubt that I have the patience.*

On my first visit I inquired about obtaining "frontier type stuff" and he showed me a catalog from Track of the Wolf. That November I told my mother about the catalog store and for my birthday she ordered a red (or rather scarlet) 4-point Hudson's Bay Blanket.

In early December of 1981, I received a catalog from Track of the Wolf along with my blanket. In the catalog, were pages and pages of muzzleloading gun parts with particularized lists for specific styles of rifles, smooth bores and pistols in well-known schools of architecture. There were all sorts of accoutrements, tools, books, knives, tents, trade silver and ornaments. On and on it went. Frankly, it was a bit overwhelming.

At the time, I had not considered the gun kit portion of the catalog relevant to me. Even though I had been making all sorts of accoutrements for myself that echoed the primitive ethic of a muzzleloading frontiersman, putting a gun together from a kit was a different matter. I had always purchased guns in ready-to-shoot condition, therefore, I had not taken the step of acquiring a muzzleloader or felt that any realistic opportunities had presented themselves.

I usually concentrated on all the books and ephemera. I had, for a number of years, been making clothing and such. To me, those projects were easy to make.

The following year, 1982, I again requested a blanket item for my birthday, but this time it was a scarlet Hudson's Bay capote.[2] In order to avoid the Christmas chaos, the folks at "Track" advised me to order it ahead of time, so I asked my mother for the garment during the summer months. It took a while, but I received the capote in mid-August or so and waited for the opportunity to use it in cold weather, which I did all that winter and into the following spring.

In the fall of 1983, I shot my first eight-point whitetail. It weighed over 190 lbs., dressed. At that time, I still did not harbor any illusions of owning a muzzleloader, but during that regular deer hunting season, I continued to wear a buckskin shirt I had made from hides that I had tanned, and over that, my scarlet capote.

I felt like a modern day mountain man, except without the muzzleloader. However, my education in black powder shooting was just around the corner. My first purchase of a front-stuffer would occur less than a year later, in the spring

The Spark

quarter of my fourth year of college, in 1984.

The Big Purchase

It was a serendipitous event thanks to a U-Do-It shop in Grand Rapids, Minnesota. I was curious about the SALE advertised on the door of the shop and, upon entering, spied a kit for a heavy, .54 caliber Thompson/Center "Hawken" caplock rifle, replete with gleaming brass furniture, including a brass patch box in the side of the stock; for only $150.00. The materials needed to sand, finish and oil the stock, as well as, clean and brown the barrel, were only about $7.00. For another $12.00 I got a pound of powder, 100 balls and patch grease. To accompany all of that, the owner of the store threw in a .530 cleaning jag[3] and brass powder flask at half-price as part of the deal. The total tally was around $180.00. How could I possibly resist the chance to own a true, working muzzleloader, and one that was made in the U.S.A.? Like a prospector who had just struck a vein of high-grade ore, my golden opportunity had finally come to fruition. In no time, I was out the door with my new acquisition.

Upon my arrival, back at the lake cabin, I cleared the kitchen table and laid out all the parts, including the directions. The next three days were spent in a myopic effort, the end result of which was a finished black powder rifle.

Following that I quickly cobbled together a chunk of wood with a dowel for a makeshift short starter, then brought all my loading stuff outside and laid it on a table. I loaded and shot the new firearm several times. I was positively giddy, but knew I had more work ahead of me. I needed to make a shooting pouch, a bag for the round balls, a more streamlined short starter and some tools, so that I was not tied to a table or bench.

I took inventory of my leather supply, made a pattern followed by cutting, trimming and sewing. Three days later I had, hanging at my side, a pouch containing round balls and equipment, further accompanied by a powder flask. I could walk anywhere and load my new smoke pole from my pouch many times. Not only was it fun to shoot, it was my ticket into the world of muzzleloading events, club shoots, camps, and rendezvous.

Shortly thereafter, I attended the monthly shoot with the local "Rapid River Gun Club," at their Warba range. In my first event I managed to win first place and received a frozen chicken. Before I had a chance to celebrate my success, one of the other shooters jokingly reminded me that I had to purchase a $150.00 gun just to win a $3.00 chicken. I reflected on the verbal jab and replied, "*Yeah, well we all have to start somewhere.*"

My First Rendezvous

On the following Monday, I was back at the University in Bemidji, Minnesota to finish out the last class for my two majors. When I called a friend, Tim "Fawn-Killer" Ewert, to inquire whether I could come over to his shop, he told me about a big camp, several hours from home. It was the National Muzzleloading Rifle Association (NMLRA) Mid-West Primitive National Rendezvous, being held southeast of Lake Mille Lacs, about 18 miles north of Mora, Minnesota. Fawn Killer gave me directions and informed me that if I got down there by Thursday morning I would have at least several days to camp and meet people before closing ceremonies on Saturday night.

I recall putting on the clothes I had made, such as my buckskin shirt, corduroy bush pants, badger hat, belt, knife

The Spark

and pouch, and my capote and lit out for the camp.

When I arrived, in between rain showers, I met several people I knew including Roger Cook, who invited me into his tipi during one of the rain showers. Actually, it had been raining off and on so much, that the event took on the moniker "The Mud-Western."

I also became fast friends with a trader, Paul Jones, from Texas, and inquired of him as to the regular proceedings of camp, so that I gained an idea of how this rendezvous and others were organized and governed.

Since I had no tent yet, when night came I slept in the back of my Toyota, Hilux truck under a fold-down camper I had made with a plywood roof and canvas sides. That first night was wet and cold. I was thankful for my wool capote as well as the foam mattress and several wool blankets. I was high and dry.

For cooking, I had brought, my cooler of food, a small gas burner, enameled frying pan and enamelware kettle. However, I discovered that I did not have to rely solely on my own provisions, or even cook, as a number of campers not only welcomed me, but invited me to sit at their fire and eat with them. I soon learned the meaning of the rendezvous term "camp-dogging it." I must have looked like a bewildered newcomer with a hollow leg.

I toured camp the following day and the sights and sounds that greeted me were more than I could have imagined in a pre-1840 camp. I devoted my morning to walking around camp, plus watching campers throw tomahawk and knife at the wooden blocks. During those rounds I made acquaintances such as Joe DeLarond, a blacksmith busy at his forge with his own brand of tomahawk. I perused all the trade goods on numerous blankets and in a number of trade tents.

As the sun climbed higher that morning and heated up the wet grass, it also substantially increased the humidity. I could feel myself sweating profusely under my buckskin shirt. At that point I wished that I had brought a cloth shirt, but I had not. I opted to spend an hour or two in the shade or under someone's awning to cool off. I headed for Paul Jones' awning where I sat watching over his trade goods as he traipsed off to work one of his trade deals.

By early afternoon, Paul had returned and I again took a stroll with my Thompson Center Hawken in hand. I saw a number of guns, arrayed on various blankets, being offered-up for sale. I had a fleeting thought of trading my own for a caplock longrifle, but I had the good sense to inquire of another seasoned camper that I had met the night before. His handle was "Crazy Jake."

After listening to his adventures in the Rocky Mountains and New Mexico clad in primitive clothing, armed with a muzzleloader, while riding a primitively accoutred horse, I concluded that he had the experience with muzzleloaders that I needed. I handed the longrifle to him and told him I was considering acquiring it in a trade. After he examined it, he found a number of things that were unacceptable.

His emphatic response was, "It's lunched!" Meaning it is essentially junk, a wall hanger and nothing more. He further counseled me to NOT go through with the trade and if I did, I would be sorely disappointed. He added, my T/C Hawken was in excellent working condition and I would get a lot of good use out of it. Otherwise, I would be constantly fighting the problems inherent in the other gun. I thanked him for his advice. Any inadequacies I may have been feeling at that time, simply withered with his counsel. I would go on to use the "Hawken" for some time after that, and he was right, it did serve me well.

After my return home, I could not help but think of the number of participants clad in a more eastern colonial type of garb from the mid 1700's, and wearing shirts of cloth. My own clothing, on the other hand, I had intentionally made in more of a western mountain man style after spending countless hours poring over the art work of notable western frontier artist, John Clymer. His art work, based upon his study of the Lewis and Clark genre and museum pieces available to document the trappers of the Rocky Mountains up through the 1840's, was invaluable and decades ahead of its time.

Even though I had a soft spot for the western subject matter, the more I thought about my own emulation of a historical man, the more I considered making garments that reflected a decidedly "eastern" colonial look.

I had also been reading the early "Sacket" series of books by well known author Louis L'Amour, which transported me in square-rigged sailing ships, to the eastern colonies amid the untamed mountains of the Appalachians, and limitless game. I felt spurred on by the same excitement that had gripped me as a boy in Northern Virginia.

To satisfy my urge for an earlier look I began several projects. First, I made a light-blue broadcloth shirt (by October, I made another in red, to be used for hunting). About mid July, that summer, I focused all efforts on another garment; a caped-buckskin hunting frock in the eastern style. I felt this was necessary in order to rehabilitate a botched buckskin shirt with short sleeves, and, thereby, put that same piece of buckskin to better use.

My Journey with Deerfoot

I ripped out the seams of the old garment, soaked it in water and I tacked it out to stretch, as I did with the other hides. It formed the back portion of what would be my new longhunter hunting frock. I made sure to put fringe on the arms and shoulders and pieced together the outer-cape over the shoulders. It closed with several antler buttons (band-sawn discs of antler which I thought were totally correct for the period, only to find out years later that such buttons have not been found in any records, ledgers or archeological finds for pre-1840. They do show up about the mid-1960's).

This new hunting frock accompanied me on many an outdoor foray, whether fishing or hunting. Now, I possessed what I saw as an iconographic garment of an eastern longhunter, and even though my rifle was from a much later time period, I was no less prepared to strike out for the wilderness.

I could also easily unbutton as well as remove the hunting frock, to reveal a much cooler cloth shirt underneath it. My new clothing provided a more versatile set-up, and following that I rarely used what had formerly been my prized home-tanned, homemade buckskin shirt.

The first, real test of my new clothes and muzzleloading gear was provided by a weekend canoe trip that fall. The two and a half day, primitive, canoe trip would take place on the Prairie River, north of Grand Rapids, MN. There were seventeen campers in nine canoes. This was the charter trip of what has continued to be a primitive outing of the North Free Trappers.

The rules were simple: No plastic, no nylon, no sleeping bags, no aluminum (except for canoes), no modern boots, no jeans. In short, only items of a pre-1840 nature. The idea of the trip was to obtain meat off of the land and

The Spark

take what was available, but bringing a meal or two of homemade breadstuffs, beans, wild rice and jerky were perfectly acceptable.

I was prepared with my newly made canvas wedge-tent, primitive clothes, eastern-style buckskin hunting frock, and blue cloth shirt. I had some miscellaneous enameled cookware for the fire, with which I was not satisfied, but at the time, it was all I had. My rations, were simple. I had some meat from a deer I had taken by archery a week earlier, a pound of wild rice, a small loaf of home made sour-dough bread and some cheese. Last but not least, I brought my T/C Hawken, with 100 round balls.

I also took advantage of the opportunity to use some No. 6 shot for hunting, however, the rifling in the barrel made for a poor shot pattern. The several birds I tried to take required another shot or flew away unscathed.

During the trip, I studied a number of muzzleloading firearms that other participants had brought with them, especially the flintlocks. There were several smooth bore trade guns and some longrifles. I asked to handle a few of them and learned that the owners started out in the same manner as I had, that is to say, with a T/C rifle or a Connecticut Valley Arms (CVA) rifle. In listening to them I got the feeling that I was going to be presented with more opportunities to obtain other muzzleloaders just as they had, but for now the T/C Hawken would fill my needs wonderfully.

One lesson from the trip had left a real impression wherein I had just purchased a box of 100 lead .530 round balls and stowed them in my shooting pouch. I realized later that I should have loaded my ball bag with roughly 28 round balls (equalling one pound) and avoid the discomfort that the remaining 72 balls (an extra 2.5 pounds) left on my neck and shoulder. The "extra" round balls could have been stored in my pack basket, canoe box or even back home.

I was beginning to feel very connected to the muzzleloading scene, but there was a caveat. The more I looked at and read about other rifles, the more I began to feel that my T/C rifle fell far outside the parameters of the common "colonial" firearm. I began to look earnestly for a rifle that would fill my desire for an earlier look and feel. There was no way I could trim the T/C-Hawken enough or stretch the heavy barrel. There was nothing functionally wrong with it. It was a good gun. The Hawken rifles produced by Thompson/Center are solidly manufactured and remain dependable work horses (even thirty-five years later), but my desire to emulate Boone and his peers, moved me, at the time, to review the many selections of long, slim, eastern rifles in Track's catalog. I was not ready to buy, but I just wanted to look.

During that same time, I made my own powder horn and shelved the Civil War era powder flask. I made the horn with a modern amendment, in that I installed a bolt and nut at the large end of the horn, where the tether attaches. I had been counseled to do this by a well meaning muzzleloading veteran. (In retrospect it was unnecessary, as filling at the spout is just as fast and can be made much more moisture resistant if not water-tight).

The horn was otherwise made with a wooden base plug secured to the horn with small tacks. The small end was scraped down to accept a strap. Lastly, it has an octagon faceted tip and wooden stopper for the spout. I hung it on my shooting bag, just over top of the flap and it served me for a number of years.

The Spark

I had my friend Mark "Rooster" Roster scrimshaw a few motifs on it to give it some subtle embellishment. My handle at the time was "Pilgrim" which I carried for a few years before being honored by the Brigade in late 1992 with the name "Three Hawks."

Just the same, that first horn also references my given name as: J. W. Hayes. That first powder horn became another milestone in my journey into history and one step closer to my emulation of an earlier time.

With every perusal of the Track catalog, my desire to own a working version of a Boone-era rifle became incrementally stronger. Though some may look at my activities as tormenting myself by dreaming of something I could not afford, the reality was that one day I would be able to afford it. Moreover, in listening to my aunts and uncle discuss classic authors one day, I was introduced to Herman Melville's statement "***Be faithful to the dreams of your youth***." Simply put, I felt it was an exhortation not to give up hope.

That hope became a reality about a year after I graduated from College. At that point all my preparations, all my prior projects, all my clothing, all my mistakes and advancements, would finally focus on what I saw as the ultimate project. It is then and there that the story of Deerfoot begins in earnest.

After perusing the catalog for several months, I spied a likely candidate. I reviewed my savings, after which, I took the plunge and purchased all the parts needed for that rifle. So began the next leg of the journey.

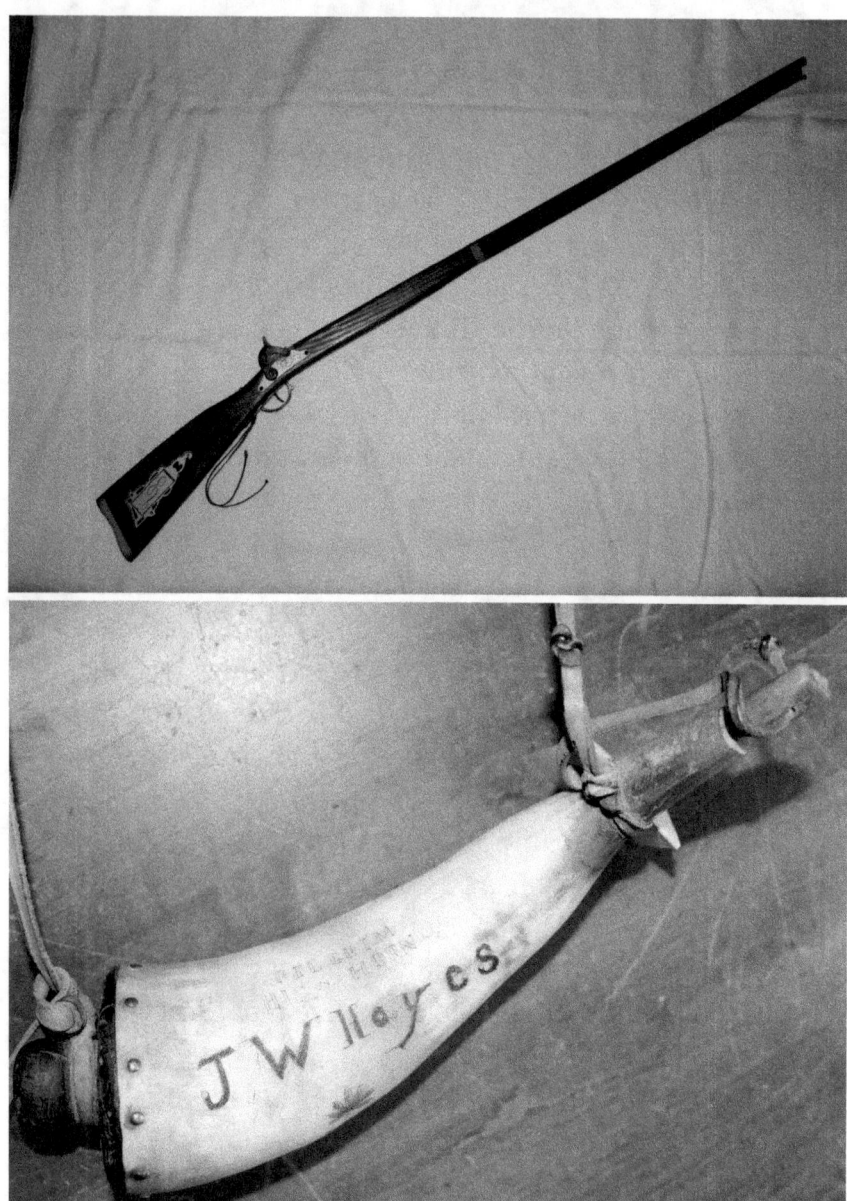

Top - Fontier Arms toy "longrifle" from childhood.

Bottom - My first powder horn which reads: **_Pilgrim His Horn, J.W. Hayes_**

The Spark

Left-Author checking beaver traps, wearing the red capote, on a primitive outing 1984.
Right-Author portaging camping items on a primitive canoe trip along the Prairie River, Northern Minnesota. T/C Hawken in hand, capote in the basket, 1984.

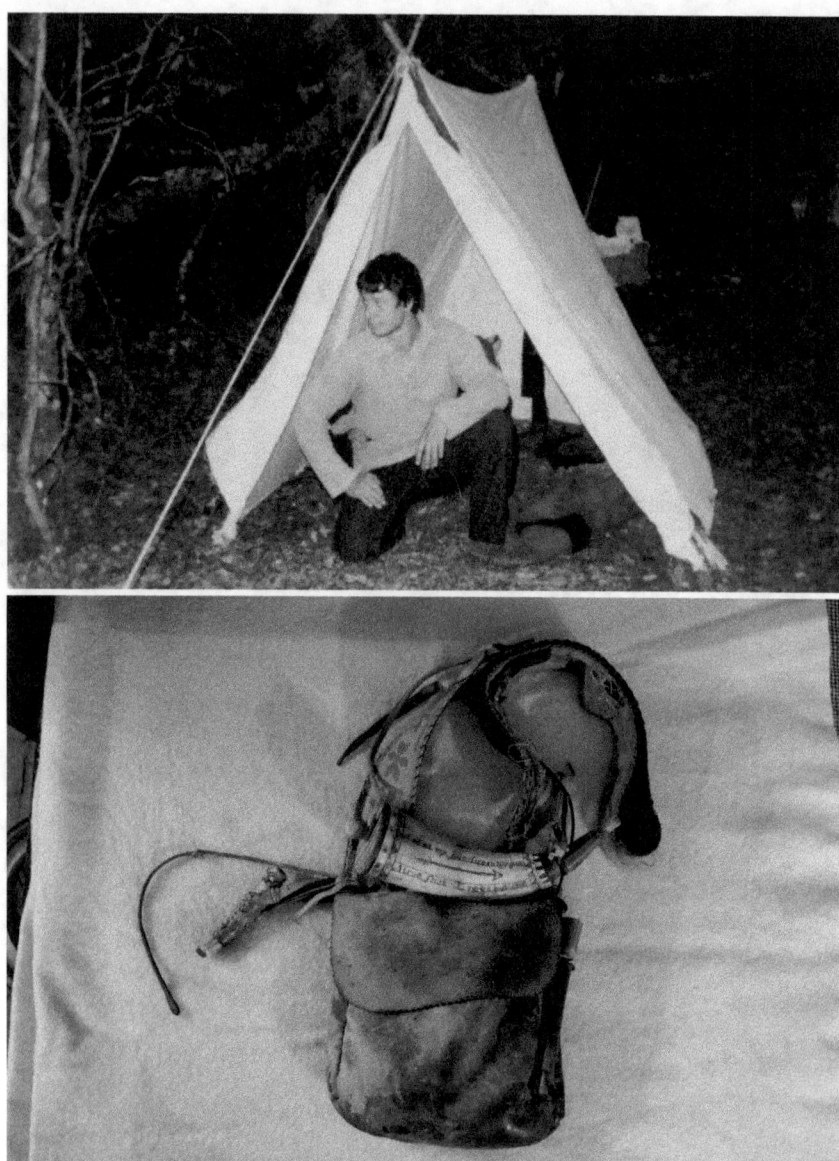

Top-My first tent, as deployed on the primitive Pairie River trip in 1984. Bottom-My first pouch made for the .54 caliber T/C Hawken. Though it serviced Deerfoot in .45 caliber, it again serves as a .54 pouch for the flintlock, Ultimus. This is the subsequent main horn on which I inscribed, *"God at my side - fire in my gun. A true shot - I need but one."* An antlered-handled moccasin awl in its case, hangs from the strap, on the left side of the photo.

Chapter 2
The Package

In early June 1985, I finished a twelve-week internship with the Environmental Protection Agency in Washington D.C. I returned to the lake cabin nestled on the banks of Sissebakwet Lake (from the Ojibwe word ziinzibakwad meaning sugar/maple sugar), in the north woods of Minnesota. Waiting for me when I arrived, was a package containing a long wooden stock, straight octagon barrel and parts for the Tennessee rifle.

I had a two week window at the cabin, before heading to my summer job as a camp counselor at the Gunflint Wilderness Camp. I was determined to use part of that time to assemble the rifle because once there, I would not have the time or the availability of nearby stores. The camp sits down river from the end of the Gunflint Trail in the Boundary Waters Canoe Area Wilderness which is seventy miles from the nearest town of Grand Marias.

I was not alone, however, as Craig, a neighbor and schoolmate of mine since first grade, accompanied me from Virginia. He and I spent the next two weeks fishing, boating, canoeing and exploring logging trails with a motorcycle, which distracted me from working on the rifle.

The truth is I felt rushed, and I was a rookie at the time. My assembly of the gun was mediocre at best. In some cases it was just poorly executed. Even though I had made a kit rifle several years earlier, this project was not really a kit, but a collection of parts with a blueprint of the intended rifle. A number of the parts, including the stock, needed considerably more attention than the effort required to assemble a boxed kit. What I lacked was experience and the opportunity to compare the assembly of other rifles with my own. This was the first of many challenges to follow.

I relied on the advice from people at the hardware stores to determine their idea of a good stain or sealant for the wood. I do not believe any of them had a clue what I was trying to accomplish. After dozens of comments and ideas I purchased what I thought would be the best combinations for my purposes. I ended up staining the maple stock with a dull opaque mixture that remains superficial to this day. It does not compliment the wood.

In drilling the holes for the pins that insert through the barrel loops, I had never seen others perform this procedure. I figured, how hard could it be? The result was, I had to drill some of the holes twice, then fill in the mistakes with birch tooth picks. When it was time to inlet the butt plate, the wood-to-metal fit was crude and I had to fill in the gaps with beeswax.

At that time, I did not know about inletting black or the traditional method of using candle soot to blacken the underside of the piece to be inlaid. By inserting and removing the piece, the soot rubs off to reveal the high-spots on the wood that need to be scraped or shaved down. Without it, a person is blindly removing wood.

There were other small areas which could have been finished more decently, but regardless of my lack of skill, that created those rough areas, it was only cosmetic and it did not affect the rifle's performance. Most importantly the finished product was indeed an eastern style longrifle.

Once assembled, I was both relieved and elated to finally have a piece of the longhunter romance, a rifle with at least the "flavor" of Boone. The long, slender muzzleloader was my connection to East Tennessee, Southeastern

Kentucky or Southwestern Virginia. I felt a sense of kinship with the hunters and pioneers of that region and the era of the early 1800's. My new longrifle mirrored the ever-present companion of the numerous characters in the historical paperbacks and novels that I so eagerly devoured. Even with all of my flaws in it, I identified with it, as though it had been some long lost relative, and saw it as my first choice for a firearm whether plinking or hunting. Moreover, I hoped the director of the camp would see the muzzleloader as a welcome addition to the shooting activities that would be provided there.

When the day of departure dawned, Craig and I packed the truck, shut the cabin and six hours later arrived at the end of the Gunflint Trail just in time for sunset. That night we slept in the truck at the edge of the Seagull River. The next morning, the director picked us up and we traveled by boat another mile to reach the camp.

Craig spent a week at the camp helping clean and, most especially, tune up a dozen Coleman lanterns used for lighting. There was no electricity in the camper's cabins; it was limited to the cook-shack and the director's cabin. This last week would round out Craig's vacation, before he headed back to Virginia, but not without leaving his mark.

On day four, after chores, I lent the rifle to Craig to shoot at the range, and within a half-hour, he accidentally broke the ramrod. Thankfully he was not hurt, but since there was no hickory on the Seagull River, my only option at that point was to cut several small whips, one of maple and the other of hazel, for use as ramrods.

The upshot of this occurrence was that it forced me to learn how to clean and straighten them by hand using the hot flame from a propane burner (steam is actually better suited to this task). Shortly after the first wave of young male and female campers arrived at the camp, I had two usable ramrods, the straightest of which was the hazel. The maple took another session or two at the flame to make it nearly as straight. I used the hazel as the main ramrod and the maple as the back-up. At that point, I felt confident enough to introduce the campers to the muzzleloader and black powder shooting.

Whenever it was my turn to go to the range for shooting exercises, I brought the Tennessee rifle, however, before I knew it, summer was nearly gone.

Those two and a half months had simply flown by. The last three days were spent cleaning buildings and shutting down the camp, after which I headed back to the cabin on Sugar Lake.

I arrived home on or about August 20, took a day to unpack, and settled into the routine there. A short time later, I attended a black powder shoot. However, a funny thing happened on the way to the shoot. I stopped on the side of the road in an effort to shoot a woodchuck, but after exiting the truck and loading the longrifle, I could not locate any percussion caps. These caps are necessary for ignition of the black powder in the barrel. Though search was made for half an hour, there were none to be found rolling around in my shooting pouch or tucked away in some remote corner of my shooting supplies. I was OUT! That left me with a charged rifle and no way to shoot it. I bid the woodchuck a lucky, happy day, re-cased the rifle and travelled on to the event, in hopes that someone there had caps for sale.

In the twenty minutes it took to drive to the club's range, I had an epiphany. If I had been shooting a flintlock, I could have primed with powder from my horn and avoid

The Package

the need for percussion caps. With a good sharp rock, I could use FFg or FFFg for ignition even if I did not have FFFFg.[4] Hmmm, this singular circumstance provoked a change in my perspective and shortly thereafter, altered the course of my career in muzzleloading.

Despite the cap dilemma, I arrived at the shoot, bought several tins of caps (100 caps per tin) and jumped into the competitions. That afternoon, I burnt up half a pound of powder and over forty round balls. For most of the competitions, I placed in the top three and was positively elated with my performance and the accuracy of the rifle.

Shortly thereafter, in the second weekend of September, I headed to a rendezvous at a place called Bock's Gun Shop, outside of Brainerd, Minnesota. I camped there in the company of an acquaintance named Uncle Zeb and his daughters along with his girlfriend. Shortly after we had set up his tipi and I had set up my homemade canvas wedge tent, it was time to participate in camp activities.

That Friday evening there was a "candle shoot," the object of which was to shoot at the candlewick with round ball, snuff out the flame but not touch the candle wax. I went stride for stride with another shooter, Bob Fanning, aka "Raven." After eleven good shots for each of us, I unfortunately skimmed the wax on the twelfth shot, but he did not. As the winner, he received a beautiful candle lantern, but since I had proved so worthy a competitor, I received a book of art by, James Bama. We both ended up with bragging rights that evening, regardless of any physical prize.

Though I had not shot a deer with that rifle yet, I wanted to do something special, but subtle, to mark it as mine. Truth is, up to that point in my life I had only taken several deer using a modern rifle and several using archery. Even so, I made a request of my good friend Eugene "Gene" Shadley, that fall, to inlet the image of a deer hoof and dew-claw marks on the cheek rest of the rifle. From that point on, the rifle took on the moniker of **Deerfoot**.

As my thoughts turned from range shooting to small game season, I decided to approach hunting differently that fall. I had resolved to hunt only with my longrifle and thereby, make meat the old-fashioned way.

I had been practicing, for quite some time, with two different loads. For deer hunting, the charge was 65 grains of FFFg and a Hornady brand .440 round ball, patched with .010 cotton shirting. For small game, the charge was 45 grains of FFFg with the same round ball and patching. To achieve the smaller load, I used a line scribed on the outside of the powder measure as a reference. I held my thumb on the line and could eyeball the powder inside, up to the line nearly every time. The streamlined approach simplified things, because there was no need to carry a second measure.

Since returning from the Gunflint Wilderness Camp, I had been working at a golf course a half mile away. I was obligated for three full days and two half days per week. During my days off I would grab Deerfoot, my shooting pouch (with plenty of round balls), a full horn of powder, and walk some 200 yards to the end of the driveway. Upon crossing the road, I slipped into the hardwoods on "Nelson's Corner" to hunt for squirrels, grouse and rabbits.[5]

I had thousands of acres at my disposal. Sometimes I would head two miles north to a wood plantation, or one mile east to the neighbor's sixty-acre woods chocked full of white oaks. I roamed the woods looking for the gray bushy-tails, and I usually came back with at least two or three

The Package

every time I went out. One morning in particular, I had six squirrels in seven shots and had hit nearly all in the eye. It was satisfying to bring home meat, but more than that, I also enjoyed the fresh air, frosty mornings and the "tea smell" of the autumn woods.

The most satisfying feeling however, was the growing connection I felt with the late eighteenth century and early "Americana." I understood that my endeavors with the longrifle were a noticeably different, challenge-filled facet of hunting activities. I would generally hunt from dawn to 10:00 am, head back to the cabin to split wood, then return to the woods again at about 2:00 p.m. I usually hunted until dark. On occasion, though, I might wander the countryside all day, from dawn to dusk.

I was excited by the new challenge of hunting with a muzzleloader as opposed to a modern firearm. The longrifle formed the foundation of my longhunter-outfit and was complimented by other gear.

My "trio" of accoutrements, consisted of my rifle with shooting bag and powder horn at my side, my knife and my tomahawk tucked into my belt. These, coupled with the moccasins on my feet, a homemade shirt, and my caped, deerskin hunting frock, I was outfitted for all day or overnight. I rarely left the house without the rifle. I was confident with it and it was a tack driver.

I also continued to use the hazel ramrod I had made during my tenure up on the Gunflint, that is, until I obtained another piece of good straight-grained hickory which was heavily oiled and polished to resist scraping and wear. The hazel, it seemed, was too soft and would wear a bit on the edge of the barrel. There was no good way to make it more resistant to scraping.

My Journey with Deerfoot

I had made those ramrods in a remote area and they continued to meet my needs, even six months later. In point of fact, I had spoken with a fellow shooter who suggested that I try using a more concentrated stream of steam on the maple rod to get the last of the curves out of it. The process took about an hour, but it really did make a difference in undoing the "memory" in the maple. With that task addressed, I felt even more "self-sufficient."

I reveled in this woodsy pursuit from a bygone era. What more could a young man ask for in his attempt to emulate the longhunter ethic of Daniel Boone and David Crockett?

For the second winter in a row, I was employed at Sugar Hills Ski Resort, across the lake from the cabin. The money I earned provided me with a new-used truck, but just as importantly, it allowed me to remain in the area. I continued to pursue primitive fall hunting and trapping activities, which included my second year attending a deer hunting camp during the muzzleloading season. The year before I could only bring my archery equipment, because my purchase of a regular firearms license had prevented me from purchasing a muzzleloader license. At that time (and until 2003), a hunter had to choose either a regular firearms license or a muzzleloader license, NOT both. This year I had a muzzleloader license in hand and I felt anxious, but also optimistic.

Sad to say, the opportunities to shoot deer were few and far between during that warm, snowless season. Moreover, the places where we could hunt were either the size of a postage stamp or had already been heavily hunted during archery and regular firearms. The end result was, what few deer remained, were on high alert, easy to spook

The Package

and hard to hunt!

After the close of deer season, I continued to use Deerfoot to hunt for small game, namely: squirrels, rabbits, grouse and the occasional nuisance porcupine. I always made sure to have several pounds of FFFg powder and several hundred round balls on hand.

I thought I was ready for anything, but time would prove me wrong. A short time later, in February 1986, our shooting club organized a winter shoot at an outdoor venue called McCormick's Store. After one of my shots on target, I was trying to dislodge the spent copper cap and I did what I always did; I "flicked" the cock by pulling it back slightly and let it go. It was a procedure born of habit, to which almost every caplock shooter resorted. The intended result was to quickly dislodged the spent cap from the hammer-cup and then jiggle it out. Only in my case on that frigid day, I succeeded in breaking off the half-cock notch from my sear. Essentially, my gun was disabled because I was no longer able to place the lock on half-cock. I felt hamstrung, nearly naked without a working rifle. I needed to get it fixed and soon.

I ordered a new sear and brought the lock to Gene Shadley for his assistance in refitting and tempering the same. It took a couple of months, but the lock was back in action by June. I had learned my lesson: "no more flicking." After that, I used a vent pick to dig the cap out of the cock and I had no more trouble with broken sear notches.

Later that summer, I stayed with my godparents, Julien and Jewel Arnquist, in South St. Paul, while studying for law school entrance exams. I took a long weekend and camped at the Mid-Western Primitive Rendezvous near LaFarge, Wisconsin a mere two hours away from the Twin

Cities.

By this time I had made many friends in the local rendezvous circuit and we all tried to camp together when possible. Since we always seemed to be within ten yards of a hooter, the group adopted the moniker, "Hooterville."

Out of this group, several teams were fielded for the competitions. We generally all shot on the line together and, as for the trail walk competition, two five-person teams originated from our Hooterville.

When my team was ready, three of us crossed the Kickapoo river on a fallen log and two others used a canoe. Following that we squirmed our way through chest-tall stinging nettle, then skirted wooded bluffs and then ran down logging trails until we were sweating profusely. All the while we were trying to avoid detection and "capture" by the young 14-year-olds who were dressed as woodland Indians. They were crawling over the area like ants, looking for us! When we crawled, our guns were in the mud and dirt. When we crossed water, it was easy to slip or trip, which meant the gun got dunked. When it came time to shoot at targets our rifles needed to work every shot, no popped caps, no clatches, so we made sure to keep them in working order.

Everyone paid particular attention to clean his gun every day due to the high humidity. Such conditions were sure to turn any left over fouling in the breech into black toothpaste. This sort of build up was sure to dampen a charge or impede the ignition altogether. After all the sweating, it was a good idea to wipe down the barrel at the end of the day and apply a bit of oil to prevent rust.

I was following the lead of more experienced shooters in these small seemingly inconsequential tasks, but when it came time to shoot the next day, they made all the difference.

The Package

It made the experience more enjoyable and I shot the rifle until I exhausted the three quarters of a pound of powder in my horn and nearly a full tin of caps. The rifle shot well, and as long as I kept it clean I had no problems. My skills were on par with a number of good shooters there, but I still had a lot to learn.

I was blessed to move in with a friend and fellow buckskinner, Paul Roster, aka "Little Crow" and his family. As a group, his family and I attended a least three rendezvous that summer. With each rendezvous, I was sure to burn up a half pound of powder and at least fifty shots. Thankfully, the prizes we won regularly consisted of more Goex FFg and FFFg powder and more round balls in Hornady's handy 25-count blister packs. Needless to say we all felt like we were shooting for free. Paul and I often conferred about the competitions, as we both shot .45 caliber, caplock, longrifles and we both hunted with them as well.

The contests ran all day long and we stayed at the shooting line until the day was over. Goex and Hornady were regular sponsors of the camps, and though we could not purchase powder at the camps, many of us returned the favor by purchasing a box of round balls in our chosen calibers.

One fortunate consequence of staying with the Rosters was, their apartment sat about three miles from Track of the Wolf in Osseo, Minnesota. We visited the establishment on a bi-weekly basis...or more.

By August 25, I headed across town to Hamline Law School on Snelling Avenue in St. Paul and began living in the dorms for my first year of law school.

Due to dorm policies which prohibited guns, I had to leave the rifle with Little Crow, or back at the family cabin, but my thoughts of being in the woods with rifle in hand were constantly in the back of my mind. I always seemed to be a week or two away from planning a hunting trip or just finishing with a hunt.

For my first five weeks of school, I had a ton of reading to get through and every night I went to bed tired and eyesore. Yes, I loved to read, but trying to distill the law from the facts of many, many cases was a bit overwhelming at first. I read and studied all day, every day and all weekend long. I looked forward to a break.

A Much Needed Adventure

When early October arrived, I attended, as in previous years, a primitive canoe trip in which there were twenty-two 17-foot canoes manned by men dressed in pre-1840 clothing. There were also two 26-foot North Canoes paddled by six men each, and in one, a woman. This year we made our way down a portion of Minnesota's Crow Wing River.

This year, as in years past, numerous wives and mothers rose before dawn to cook a breakfast of bacon, eggs and pancakes and then saw us off.

All the canoes had been loaded onto one of several trailers the night before and the shuttle trucks set a course for a convenient bridge. Upon arrival at the drop-off point each team removed their canoe from the trailer and carried it to a spot along the water's edge, accompanied by their gear and bedding. In no time, there were eight canoes and their respective cargo lining the river bank. As the canoes were loaded and balanced, each person sorted out where a particular piece of gear, pack or box would be positioned in their own canoe and yet have ready access to firearms and accoutrements. The mass flotilla got under way in the early morning well before 9:00 a.m., just as the frost was melting.

The Package

I took the stern, and Little Crow occupied the bow. Once we shoved off, we floated and paddled for a time as we made small adjustments.

For my own purposes, Deerfoot, still in its blanket case, lay to my right over the thwart in front of me with the barrel down and the wrist tied onto the same thwart. I had my shooting bag looped over and secured to the thwart as well. It was going to be an hour or so before we reached any sort of hunting territory so there was no need for immediate access to our rifles.

Little Crow wore his hunting pouch on his side and had the butt of his rifle still in the blanket case under his seat and the barrel pointed over the bow, in which situation he managed to paddle for about ten minutes before he changed his plan. Since he was dripping too much water on the gun case, he opted to turn the gun around and to a position behind his left arm and tucked it in between the cargo and the port side of the canoe.

After our "shake-down" we continued to paddle for at least an hour as we stayed in the company of a collection of our friends in other canoes. Our particular group of several canoes included both of the big canoes, one owned by "Fawn Killer" and the other by one of the local brigades. In another canoe were (the late) Don "Stray-Bull" Bronz and Mark "Sticker" Luneburg. In another canoe was Dave "Z" Zaeski and Paul's brother, "Rooster."

It was a colorful sight as most of the folks had begun the voyage wearing their capotes made of Hudson's Bay or Witney Blankets, in a range of colors, namely: red, green, white, blue, as well as striped. In addition to the capotes most wore wool lined moccasins, and caps of wool or fur.

Even though the air was chilly, it did not take long for

those who were paddling to warm up, and soon the capotes came off to reveal a myriad of buckskin shirts and coats, linen hunting frocks and those who opted for lighter wool shirts.

Some canoes lagged behind while others maintained a faster pace, and were soon out of sight. Little Crow and I paddled steadily as the terrain changed from muskeg and lowland swamp with clumps of willow, to higher ground with a prevalence of hardwoods.

There was a good deal of general conversation about history and the river itself. Little Crow and I enjoyed the historical canoe trip, especially in the good company of other like minded individuals.

We continued to keep pace with the group for some time, that is, until we entered a thick stretch of oaks, then we were "all eyes" as we scanned the surrounding landscape more thoroughly. It was only a matter of time before we found a stretch of habitat that was just too promising to pass up.

We bid our friends adieu for the time being, and glided over to the edge of the river. After we brough the canoe parallel to the bank, I took hold of some brush with my right hand. As soon as canoe was firmly against the bank, Little Crow grabbed his gun and crawled out and up the bank. After laying down his gun, he held the canoe steady while I donned my shooting pouch. I untied my rifle and handed to him. He walked the rifles over to a flat piece of ground and leaned them against a white oak, then returned to hold the canoe for me and I likewise crawled up, onto the bank. After securing the canoe to a good sapling on the river's edge, I stepped over towards the white oak and the guns. I believe we both sported broad grins as we removed

The Package

our guns from their blanket cases. In no time at all our trusty rifles were loaded, capped and ready for business.

Having two people hunting squirrels is a ready method for encouraging them to move from their hiding spots. As one hunter stays put, the other can circle around a tree whereupon the squirrel focuses on the moving hunter. Invariably the squirrel will attempt to keep the tree between itself and the moving hunter. As the squirrel changes its position it becomes more shootable by the stationary hunter.

At that first stop we heard several squirrels barking, at which point Little Crow and I employed the two person technique. Within several minutes, the squirrels had not only revealed their positions, but were jumping through the tree tops. We had no choice except to follow them, hoping they would pause and stay put, in order to provide us with a non-moving target. Since we were both using round ball, we wanted unobstructed shots at the head.

We chased one which refused to stop until it finally came clambering down an ironwood, and quickly darted into a hole about three feet off the ground. We waited very quietly for a good ten to fifteen minutes with no talking. When he poked his head out of the hole I was braced for the shot and took him.

I had no sooner reloaded when another moved to a crotch. Little Crow, holding his rifle aloft in his right hand, with his left outstretched like a wing, excitedly and quickly changed his position like a quarterback looking for an opening as he skipped sideways over the dry leaves. He found a sapling where he braced up. Seconds later his rifle boomed and the squirrel came tumbling down with a thump a mere foot from the river's edge.

With all the commotion of shooting and moving

through the dry brush we inadvertently rousted a raccoon from its den in a large hollow oak. It clawed its way up into the thin branches of a maple tree where it looked down on us, probably with some disdain. Since the season on raccoons had not opened, we left it to its lone, high, lofty vigil and headed back to the canoe.

When we got under way again there were no other canoes in sight. We, like the raccoon, maintained our place on the river as a single canoe. We paddled for a good twenty minutes and finally managed to see one canoe off in the distance at the other end of a straight stretch of water, so we were not too far behind. We did not try to catch up, however, as there was a lot more ground to hunt and we were in no hurry.

On our next stop we each donned our red capotes as the thick cloud cover made the damp air a bit more chilly. We each headed in opposite directions on the bank, amid tall oaks, maples and basswoods. When my partner was just out of sight, I heard something walking in the leaves, so I positioned myself behind a large birch. Peering around the tree I spied a grouse walking in my direction; perhaps investigating me as some large, red object that had invaded his turf. From my cover, I raised the barrel to sight-in on his neck, promptly touched off the charge and immediately I had one grouse flopping in the leaves like a drummer. That sound coupled with our walking around unnerved a nearby squirrel, prompting it to bark. I located the squirrel, waited for it to show its head and seconds later, the rifle boomed. The squirrel tumbled out of the tall tree and landed on the ground with a thump.

After reloading, I walked down a small incline to retrieve my quarry, when I noticed the unmistakable heart-

The Package

shaped leaf of the wild ginger plant inches from my foot. I procured a stout stick and dug down a few inches and gently removed the finger sized root from the soil. After knocking off the dirt, I wrapped it in a piece of cloth and placed it in my belt pouch. Perhaps I would be able to use it to season the grouse I had just bagged.

Before two o'clock that day I had secured my "hunt or starve" rations. My intrepid friend with his own .45 longrifle also managed to end the day with a second squirrel. We arrived at the camp site to find at least eight or nine camp fires already going. Our camp-mates Sticker and Stray Bull had saved us a spot at their fire which already had a good bed of coals going. Little Crow and I used a frying pan to cook our squirrels in bacon grease.

While we waited on the squirrels, the four of us shared a bottle of Sticker's home-made wheat wine which hit the spot. We enjoyed good food and good company at the fire and that night we slept soundly.

The next morning, using the wild ginger root I had dug the day before, along with some salt and pepper, I gently boiled the grouse until it was barely done. It came out tender, like lobster tail, and I shared part of it for breakfast. When the coffee in our kettle was gone, we tore down camp, loaded the canoes and headed down river to our pick-up point.

At the time, we gave no thought to the fact that our rifles were caplocks. We were reveling in our outdoor muzzleloading activities and feeling like woodsy shooters. It had been a good weekend, made all the better by the fact that my friend and I had, on several occasions, "made meat" with our longrifles.

Soon our grand adventure was over, and we headed back to the Twin Cities and Little Crow's apartment. After unloading his truck we took about fifteen minutes to clean our rifles as we conferred about our successful canoe trip. All good things come to an end, and a short time later it was time for me to leave my rifle and other stuff at the apartment and get going. As I headed back to school, I felt proficient as a hunter, and blessed to have shared my weekend with good friends.

Ruminating on an Image

When I was not inundated with reading case law, I rested my eyes, and occasionally, day-dreamed about longrifles and the men who wielded them. It all seemed so romantic and yet it felt like something was missing.

The thing that kept nagging at me during that year, was the mental image of the long, trim, graceful lines of the rifle, but the mental image was not a caplock. In my mind's eye, I saw a *flintlock* which my rifle did not possess. The image seemed to summon up thoughts of the proper ignition system which, of course, Daniel Boone and his contemporaries employed to fire their longrifles. Ever since the "woodchuck incident" the year before, the image of a flintlock provoked a growing restlessness within me.

During my considerations, I lamented that I had not simply ordered my rifle as a flintlock. After all, I would not be in the position now to go through the work of changing over the ignition system. However, I also considered that I had ordered the rifle as a caplock because that is what I knew at the time. The caplocks, on both Deerfoot and the T/C, had allowed me to gain experience by shooting at many different venues and, therefore, it should go without saying, that I had developed a comfort with muzzleloaders. Now, however, I was ready to move on and give the flintlock ignition a try. My investigations began with the question, *"What would it take to replace the Siler caplock with a flintlock?"*

My presence of mind to consider a more primitive means of ignition on my firearm, however, also gave me the freedom to ponder other changes to my outdoor "historical outfit." My strong desire to reach a more serious level of participation at rendezvous, led to plans for expanding my camp amenities to include a tipi. At that time, the reality was, our deer hunting camps, fall camps and summer rendezvous all centered around using tipis for our shelters.

Many of the tipi owners I knew also had flintlocks; a sort of expected progression. Thus, the seeds of a "more serious" approach actually began with my earnest consideration of using a flintlock ignition, that is to say, the willingness to change and experiment.

At the end of the first semester, I headed back home to the cabin for the Christmas holiday and a month long break, but not before stopping at the S.R. Harris Fabric Warehouse, in Brooklyn Park, MN, to obtain some sort of fabric that would work for making a tipi. Yes, I was gearing up for a change to my firearm, but there would be a slight diversion.

My Journey with Deerfoot

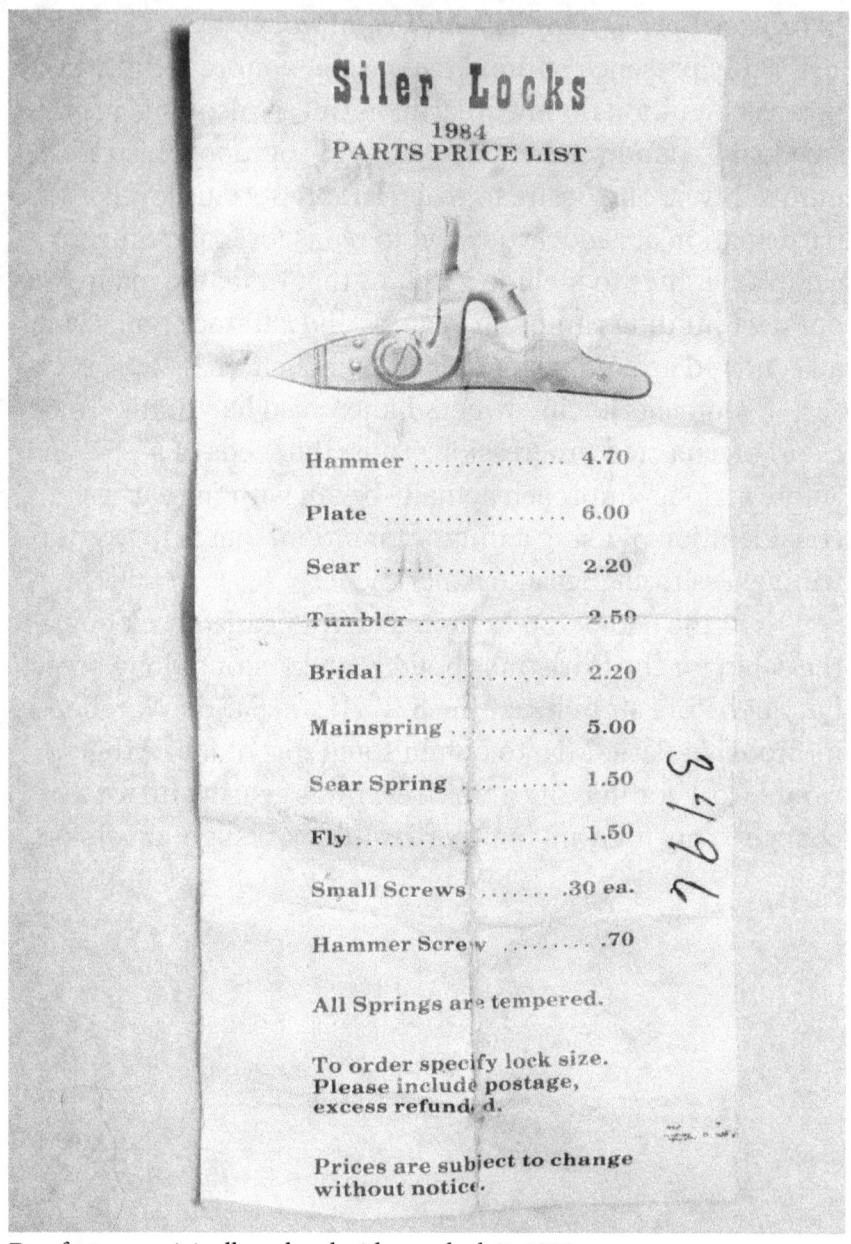

Deerfoot was originally ordered with a caplock in 1985.
An original parts list from 1984 which was, at the time, included with finished locks as well as with the lock kits. This has a good depiction, at the top, of the caplock itself. Copyright C.E. Siler acquired by Jim Chambers Flintlocks Ltd.

The Package

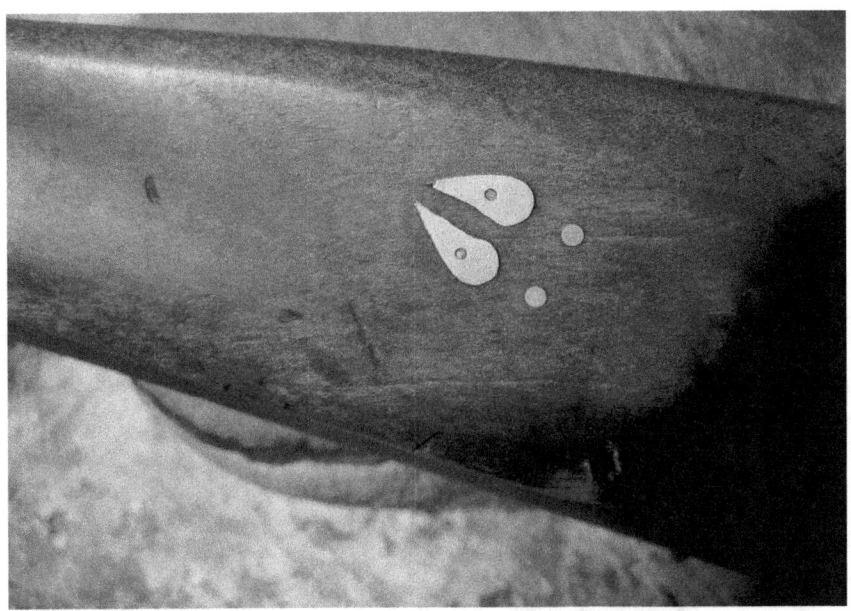

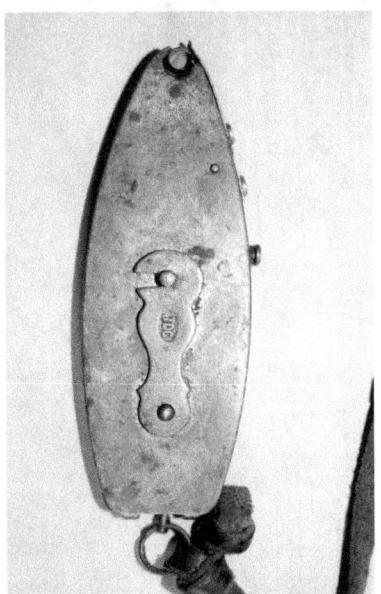
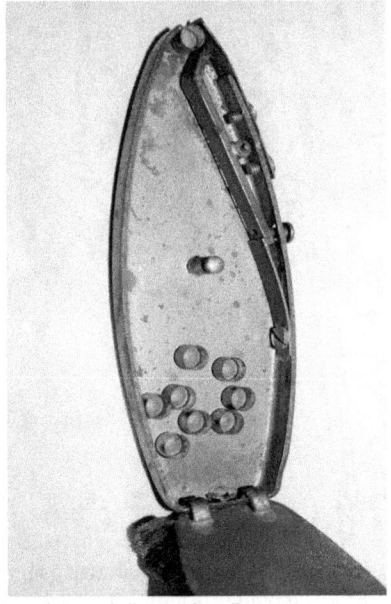

Top-The German Silver inlay of the deer hoof, hence "Deerfoot."
Bottom: Left-A spring-loaded brass capper, manufactured by Ted Cash (TDC) with lid closed, latch locked in place. (The Author's from 1984.)
Right-The open lid reveals caps with one "in-the-mouth" ready to deploy. These are popular and handy among caplock shooters, but unnecessary for flintlocks.

My requisite knife and tomahawk as part of my trio of equipment, back then. The 6" knife blade (resembling a cutlass) made by Bob Odegaard of Bemidji, was cut from a snowmobile leaf spring. The handle is rosewood, secured by: 20th Century-cutler's rivets, brass hilt and solid brass pommel. The sheath utilizes modern chromed compression rivets. The tomahawk head was commercially made. It was purchased via catalog from Golden Age Arms. Handle is of straight grained maple, and figure is "feather-grained" with leather dye.

The Package

Top-Fellow campers "Stray Bull" in the stern with his dog Mitzi riding on the cargo. "Sticker" is in the bow.
Bottom-Near canoe in foreground "Z" in the stern and "Rooster" in the bow. Upper left-background is "Fawn Killer's" 26' North Canoe, upper right background is the other 26' North canoe.

March 1988 at the Barn (owned by Bob and Wanda Odegaard) in La Port, MN. Front left to right: author, with Deerfoot, kneeling is "Rooster," Deb Bernt (now Offerdahl), far right is Paul, "Little Crow" Roster. Standing in rear unknown. Photo Courtesy Derek Olson.

Chapter 3
The Tipi Diversion

As if I needed one more thing to do, something inside of me thought it was quite necessary to pick this time to "build a new house" in the form of a nomadic dwelling. Which begs the question, *"What in the world does a tipi have to do with a flintlock?"*

In retrospect it was the first of several stepping stones in my effort to become better acquainted with my chosen exploration of historical life ways.

As I had alluded to earlier, tipis had been a part of my experience early-on, from the first rendezvous as well as fall camps, deer hunting and demonstrations with the public. The thought of finally having my own tipi was exciting.

I began by reading the **The Indian Tipi**, *Its History, Construction and Use*, **By Reginald and Gladys Laubin.**[6] As for the size, I considered either a sixteen or eighteen foot. Next, I determined how much fabric that would take to complete it without skimping.

I had heard about a fabric warehouse in Brooklyn Park, MN, on the outskirts of Minneapolis, but had not been there until I decided to make a visit on my way home. I was hoping to see, within its walls, some sort of fabric that would suffice for my project. On my visit I found some lighter fabric which would work and yet was tough enough to provide me with a decent covering. There was a bolt and a half available. I had the funds to purchase all of it and did so.

In order to make sure I was using a good pattern, I located a spot in the yard and driveway, set a pin as the top of the tipi and then (like a human compass) walked in an 18 foot semi-circle which I marked with stakes. The longest swath was the flat side of the semi-circle, (i.e. for the front), at thirty-six feet plus extra for a hem. I then measured by the width of my fabric to determine the size of each of the smaller swaths until I had "filled" the area, and reached the tangent at the other side of the half-circle.

As long as I measured out my fabric in each of the descending layers, I simply had to mark and baste them from the middle and sew outwardly. Once I had that figured out, I cut out the necessary pieces and began sewing on an old, heavy-duty Wards sewing machine that my Aunt Marge had given to me. For two weeks I worked on sewing the main cover, then the smoke flaps, and especially reinforcing at the top and front. Eventually each piece was added to the growing cover until it all came together.

My other chores while at home consisted of cutting wood for the stove and the occasional hunting foray. Soon it was time to get back to St. Paul and begin my second semester at school.

With the Easter break, I headed back to the cabin and began on the hand work of sewing the "lacing-pin" holes for the front of the lodge, but I would not be ready to set it up until I had acquired the tipi poles. I would need eighteen of them for a proper set-up (three poles for the tripod, four for the north side, four for the south side, four for the back which included the lift-pole; one for each smoke flap and a front pole outside to which the bottoms of the smoke flaps are connected).

My next task fell to fellow camper, "Stray Bull" whom I hired to cut and de-bark some spruce and balsam poles. This would be the best time to cut new poles as it was coming into spring when the bark would be full of sap, loose and hence the easiest to remove. Then the only thing to do was

The Tipi Diversion

to pick up the poles when they were done. Hopefully I could have the tipi ready for the upcoming summer line-up of events.

Back at school, I had checked out the book **Across the Wide Missouri**, by Bernard DeVoto[7], which focused on the western mountain man and the fur trade of the first and second quarters of the Nineteenth Century. The book caught my eye because I had seen a movie by the same name starring Clark Gable. Apparently the movie was shot using vintage muzzleloaders and good shooters who knew how to load and shoot which provided a number of good scenes.

Aside from the typical shooting competitions I read about other curious contests. I was fascinated by one particular game in which the mountain men participated in, such as; a tug-of-war eating contest using a 25 foot length of *boudin* (today we would call it an empty intestine used for sausage casing).

Each contestant would try to eat his way to the center and in the process bite down and pull the boudin out of the opponent's mouth (and stomach). Though it might seem to the twenty-first century person as an odd and detestable way of "letting off steam," when these hardy souls got to the rendezvous, neither the contestants nor the other camp go'ers saw anything gross with these games. What's more, the on-lookers would bet on the outcome!

I was inspired by the stories of the Western hunters and trappers, (whose feats of survival and uncanny ability to get themselves out of a jam: on steep mountains and in dark timber) that became a part of the folklore. They managed to keep their powder dry in their guns, and ready for a shot, whether it was rain, sleet, snow or bitter cold.

In reading, I thought about my own efforts to get out

into the wilds and care for my gun so it would be ready to shoot regardless of the weather. As I continued to read, I felt as though I was incrementally getting into my element, from clothing, to firearms, and now to shelters. DeVoto's descriptions allowed my thoughts to wander and imagine myself participating in the activities of those intrepid hunters and travelers of the day.

The more I read the more I could not wait to finish my tipi, head out to the rendezvous camps, and participate in the varied competitions as a more serious participant.

After the conclusion of final exams, I headed back home to Cohasset. A day after settling in, I called Stray Bull to check on the progress of the tipi poles only to be told they were still several weeks out. At that point there was some fishing to do as well as work on a lock project for Deerfoot.

Several weeks later many of us attended a rendezvous wedding, where I finally received my tipi poles. Though we were going to do some shooting on the day prior to the ceremony, I instead opted to get my lodge set up for the first time. The ever-helpful "Rooster" agreed to lend a hand to mark the poles and arrange the cover for the set-up. After several hours of marking the poles, tying and re tying the tripod, which also required setting and resetting the poles, we were ready for the final set-up.

The tripod was set up with a door pole, south pole and north pole. In tying the tripod the foot of the door pole is set to the east, and the feet of the south and north poles are set to the south. The north and south poles are tied underneath of the door pole at their apex. When the tripod is lifted the door pole and south pole stay in their footed place, and the north pole is swung to the north for its footing. In order to face the door easterly, the "door pole" is to the south of the

The Tipi Diversion

door opening, and the first pole of the next four in the set becomes the other door pole.

Starting with that pole to the north of the door, these next four (1-4) are placed in succession, rounding toward the "north pole of the tripod and into the opening at the top.

The next four poles (5-8) are placed to the south of the "door pole" in succession, rounding toward the "south pole." The next four poles (9-12) start to the south of the "north pole." Two poles (9&10) are placed in succession, but a space is skipped (11) for the lift pole and then the last pole (12) is set. The poles are wrapped four times and the rope staked to the ground, and then the lift pole (11) is used to lift the canvas into place. *see figure below*

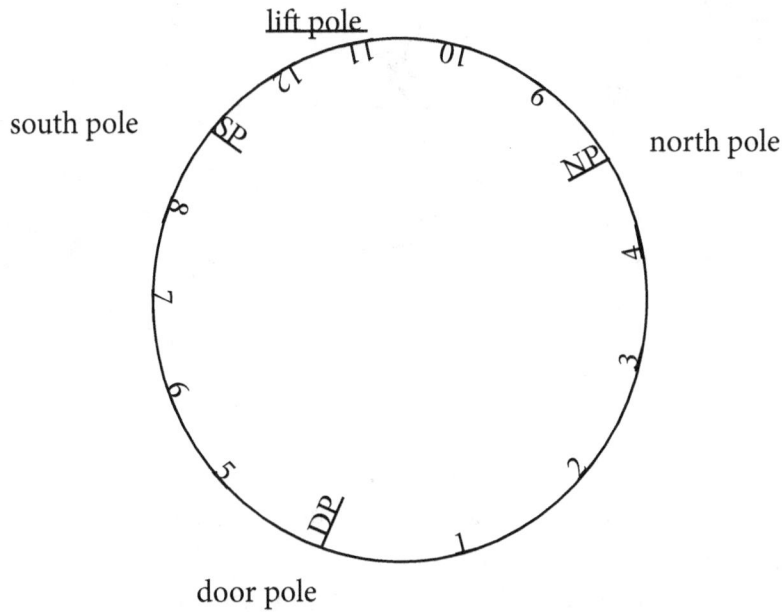

At last, we lifted the canvas into place, and unrolled it onto the rest of the poles. The front was tied to hold it followed by inserting the lacing pins down the front.

Above: Lacing pins applied to close the cover of the tipi. They run from the smoke flap opening to the door and include two below the door. Tipi owner Jeremy Duckwitz.

Following that, Rooster and I made sure to pull the cover towards the ground to take out as much stretch in the fabric as possible.

We followed up by marking and trimming the bottom of the cover in order to keep the bottom of the cover about four to six inches off the ground. The liner, which is placed inside the poles will be flush with the ground, and create a space between it and the cover. This space is essential to create a draft between the cover and the liner to carry the smoke, (from the fire inside) out through the smoke flaps. We then marked the spots for the tie-loops just above the base of the cover.

All that was left to do was to cut lengths of 3/8 rope into two foot sections and tie the ends together. The loops were attached by inserting rocks or round balls into the fabric and cinching the tie loop around them using a clove hitch. Stakes were run through the loops, then the loops were twisted to cinch them around the stakes after which they were pounded into the earth. The result was a taut canvas cover.

Following the work on the cover, I stepped inside to string a quarter-inch rope from pole to pole. Starting at the first pole, about 4 ft. from the ground, I continued the rope to the second and made one wrap around that pole and continued to do so until I had the rope strung all the way around and back to the starting point. By wrapping the rope from the inside of the pole around to its "outside" and then around to the inside the rope remained three to four inches from the cover. At the underside of each pole where the rope wrapped around a given pole I inserted two pegs about an inch apart, so the rain water that ran down the inside of the poles would be channeled between the pegs and continue down to the ground. These are called "rain-pegs."[8]

The liner was tied to the rope and the bottom of the liner was then tied to the base of each of the poles. At last, my new tipi was ready for living and it was time to move in.

In a prominent place over my bedding area hung Deerfoot along with my shooting bag. I could now cook

Above: Rain pegs applied to the inside of the pole within the tipi.

and tend to my camp needs as well as my rifle during any weather, any season. Though the tipi was not exactly within the Daniel Boone/colonial ethic, I was elated to have a camp that echoed my dedication to primitive camping.

Many of the people I knew who were serious about rendezvous and historical life ways owned or had owned a tipi. With my new acquisition, I too felt like I had finally attained a satisfying level of accomplishment for my camp.

The Tipi Diversion

Author's tipi on its first set-up at a camp. The nearly symmetrical upright conical shape is more akin to a Sioux style tipi; the front and back have similar angles. The liner, which reaches to the ground, can be seen below the cover. The cover does not reach to the ground, to allow for draft. The smoke flaps at the top of the cover are open to the front. The front door generally faces to the East.

Inside of tipi. The liner is visible with Deerfoot, still in its case, suspended above the bed with shooting pouch hanging below. A fire burns in the pit ready to cook a meal. The liner rope can be seen reaching from pole to pole.

Top-College roommate, Rick Kuntz, seated, shares conversation with a young T.J. Roster in front of the Author's tipi at the Rapid River Rendezvous, Warba MN, in early August 1987. Other tipis can be seen in the background.
Bottom-Author's tipi in the foreground with door open, amid dozens of other tipis at a High Plains Rendezvous held at Fort Ransom, ND, June 1987.

Chapter 4.
The Conversion Begins

My first essential task, was to make sure that the new flintlock would interchange with the percussion lock that was in Deerfoot. Thankfully, Siler locks are interchangeable, so that the flintlock plate and mechanism would fit into the lock mortise of the stock without any retro-fitting.

Secondly, the drum-bolster [9] could be removed from the side of the barrel, and a touch-hole liner should fit into that same threaded opening. The liner is important because the liner has a hole in the center which creates the touch-hole through which the flash in the pan ignites the powder in the barrel.

Thirdly, I could use the same lock-screw and thread size as that of the former caplock. The more I analyzed the conversion, the more excited I became. The flintlock lock-plate would, in fact, fit into the lock mortise of Deerfoot without any further alterations. As May of 1987 inched closer, I could feel the anticipation well up within me.

When I visited Track, I discovered the price of completed locks was a bit out of my price range at $55.00. They did, however, stock all the pieces necessary to make a complete lock, too. Perhaps I could purchase one or two parts every couple of weeks, then work those parts into the lock; an option that would cost over $30.00. However, they also stocked flintlock kits, which, at the time; were just under $24.00, came with all the necessary parts and directions to boot.

Further, in making the lock from a kit, I would familiarize myself with the inner mechanisms. It was a win-win situation as it was both cheaper and more convenient.

My Journey with Deerfoot

This purchase occurred several weeks prior to final exams that year, so rather than becoming distracted by this technical project, I focused on school. Before long, the exams were over. My first year was done. Ah, what a relief!

When I finally arrived back home in Cohasset, I intended to take advantage of the window of time (waiting on tipi stuff), and focus on the lock conversion in earnest. I had, after all, spent the last eight to nine months, ruminating on removing the caplock and replacing it with a flintlock. Now it was time to "fish or cut bait" as they say. For the present I had a reprieve from other distractions. I excitedly began the challenge of assembling the parts in the kit.

The first tool I purchased was a drill and tap for a 10-40 thread.[10] I dug through an old steel brewery box that held my great-grandfather's tools and retrieved a handle with a chuck to hold the tap. It seemed appropriate; because it was an old tool, and I was, in essence, converting an old style rifle to an even older style. Every hole was gently bored and threads tapped according to the directions, which listed at least five different drill sizes.

When it came time to temper the lock parts, such as the sear and the frizzen (also known historically as the battery), I enlisted the help of a welder in La Prairie, MN by the name of Dick, who understood the nuances of hardening steel by quenching in oil versus quenching in water. Next, he showed me the process of "running the colors" in the steel, a process which draws the hardness back to make the piece less brittle, and more durable, but when struck with the edge of a flint, the steel will still throw sparks.

Upon assembly, I tried out the lock with the only flint, or rather rock, that I had in my possession. That particular rock was a poor sparker at best. I began to think my decision

The Conversion Begins

to change to a flinter was a mistake. My endeavors were not without a little embarrassment either.

During my initial shooting trials with my new lock as the ignition source, I went down the road to an out-of-the-way sand pit. It was not, however, far enough from view of the road. While there, getting ready to begin testing, one of the neighbors drove by with a cadre of kids and friends. They watched as I pulled the trigger about seven times resulting in seven clatches.[11] So far... NO boom. I could hear their snickers and giggling. Finally, they got bored and drove off. Once again, left to myself, I kept at it and finally I got a good spark and the rifle fired with a good loud crack. About ten seconds following my shot, I could hear another vehicle approaching from the other direction and stop. It was the neighbor and company again. Somebody commented loudly, "I can see why they quit using those things a long time ago." I stood there and suffered the slings and arrows of their taunts and laughs. Just as quickly, they left again.

Before loading another shot, I began at that moment, to obtain a better edge on the rock to cut the steel and produce a more pronounced spark. I knapped the flint as best I could and the next six or seven shots cracked off at the first pull of the trigger. Though I felt vindicated by the instantaneous ignitions, it all happened, of course, when nobody else was watching. Ah, such is life, but regardless of the embarrassment, I was determined to persevere.

A week or so later, at the monthly shoot, I sought out a trader and purchased from him a half-dozen good, black English flints of the proper size, all with keen edges. When I fitted one into the jaws of the cock and secured it, I headed to the shooting line. From the first shot and all those that followed, I had great sparks immediately and lightening-quick ignitions. The shots cracked off in succession at least eighteen or more times before I experienced a hang-fire.[12]

Moreover, one of my comrades admonished me not to overfill the pan with powder. Firstly, it will not close correctly and with ignition it creates fowling more quickly. It will build up in the pan, cling to the bottom of the frizzen, and the side of the barrel. After a few shots, it may obscure the touch hole. Rather, use only enough to fill the pan.

Secondly, make sure the frizzen hinged down to fit flatly on the pan which in turn will prevent the powder from leaking out. I also viewed a few shooters who were wiping the frizzen and flint with a piece of cloth to clear the fowling off of those places. These were all good bits of information!

Just when I thought I had it all "figured out," I began to see other horizons and consider paths that were more centered on living history. One such horizon was my use of horns. At this point I carried two horns, one for loading, one for priming.

I did this because I thought it was the best practice to use only priming powder for the pan and larger powder for the charge. The second horn (priming horn) was also of my own manufacture.

When Rooster helped me at the rendezvous wedding, I showed him the little horn that I wanted scrimshawed to dress it up a little. He had already done some scrimshaw on my larger horn, and now I was hoping he could also do my smaller horn.

Thus, for a number of years, I carried two horns, one larger for my main charge filled with FFFg to load in the barrel, and a smaller filled with FFFFg for priming the pan. I would continue to carry two horns until, on one hunt, I lost my priming horn.

The Conversion Begins

That particular horn that I had lost was a prize from a blanket shoot several months earlier. My only choice that afternoon, deep in the woods, was to prime with the FFFg powder from the big horn and it worked just fine. From that point forward, I began to load and prime with just the powder in my main horn, which approach, I have found to be more streamlined and less cumbersome. I never really used a priming horn after that, but I still have both the horns that Rooster scrimshawed for me. I cherish both horns, as person might cherish a collection of hard-fought-for merit badges.

As my experience with the flintlock expanded, I was more determined than ever to use this rifle as my main gun. There were half a dozen more canoe trips, walking trips, horse rides and various hunts and monthly shoots which gave me plenty of opportunities to shoot Deerfoot as a "flinter." There were; however, new storms on the horizon.

Not all of my muzzleloader-hunting companions thought my switch to flint was practical. When I missed any shot, whatever the reason, these same companions viewed the flintlock as an ineffective, poor choice for hunting. To them, my use of a flintlock made little sense, when I could have used, as they saw it, a "more reliable" caplock ignition. They seemed offended, and accused me of being an elitist.

The caustic comments flew from their lips, *"You might just as well throw that #*@^%$ "flinch-lock" at the critter!"*

Another said, *"Get yourself a REAL gun and leave that #*@^%$ flinter at home!"*

I recall one small game hunt with three other acquaintances, one of whom was a die-hard caplock shooter. We headed to a grand oak ridge and shot several squirrels apiece. However, it began to rain just as I took aim on a bushytail. It was an easy target, but due to the occasional drizzle and high humidity, I experienced a "flash-in-the-pan." [12] So, I re-primed the pan amid incessant ridiculing from the one companion about how "reliable" my rifle was, especially when I flashed a second pan with no ignition.

He firmly elbowed me out of the way, stepped forward with his caplock and took the squirrel in the head. *"Good thing we had a caplock to back up the flinter,"* he said in a heavy tone of derision.

I felt that the comment was harsh and unnecessary. It seemed that his ridicule was intended to shame me into stop using a flintlock. Instead of assuming a sense of guilt or shame, however, I chose to press on and view the ignition as a learning opportunity. It provoked a growing curiosity on how to avoid such ignition failures in the future.

What had started with a sharp remark, made me pause and ruminate on a number of questions, the first of which was, "What did the early hunters do to protect their locks from precipitation?" The first of many lessons that began to take shape, was my realization of the additional utility of the cape on a hunting frock. Afterwards, regardless of how warm it was, I endeavored to use a caped hunting frock to cover the lock and protect the breech area from precipitation, but the search for alternatives did not stop there.

The next lesson, and caveat, occurred when I used my open blanket capote to cover the lock area, while getting into the deer stand. Maneuvering in the cramped tree stand was difficult and once in, I could not stand so I sat. In my efforts, I had inadvertently allowed snow to fall on the exposed lock area, which melted and dampened my charge and prime.

When two deer came into view, I tried a shot, but experienced a hang-fire. Needless to say, I missed the deer.

The Conversion Begins

I had to remain seated so reloading took a while and by the time I was ready for a second shot, the deer were gone. I had only myself to blame for this miss and I actually dreaded going back to camp. Once again, when everyone came together, I endured more scorn and cutting ridicule, *"Well, that's what you get when you use a !*@&#&$% 'flinchlock' buddy!"*

My one consolation was the fact that I had put my sights on a deer. That would have to do for now. I may have been discouraged, but I was undaunted.

In the several years that followed, I learned to ignore the incessant attempts, by some folks, to dissuade me from using a flintlock. Now they openly accused me of being an elitist and how my education was getting in the way of my common sense. *How ridiculous*, I thought. After all, it was my choice.

Finally, I quit hanging around them. If I had listened to them, I would never have continued my journey to become as familiar with a flintlock as other folks are with car engines. What I wanted though, was answers; even if I did not know the questions.

I have often heard it said of an antique firearm, *If that gun could only talk, what tales would it tell?* Guns, as we know, cannot speak. There is also no way to ask questions of a two hundred fifty-year-old colonial man either.

My intention was to gain an understanding of things that Boone and his contemporaries did not have to think about. In other words, things that were second nature to a colonial hunter, soldier, militiaman and farmer, relative to handling a flintlock long gun. A good example of second nature in the 21st century would be the exchange,

"Don't put your finger in a light socket!"

This would be followed by the response: "Well obviously, if you do not want to get electrocuted, everyone knows that."

The words "obviously" and "everyone knows that," belie the treatment of light sockets as second nature to a citizen of the 21st century. It seems intuitive, a type of behavior which is natural for those of us who use electricity every day to avoid being jolted by 120 volts.

Though my familiarity with the longrifle began as a caplock, it had progressively changed to a flintlock. The conversion was another important mile marker on that path and gave me my first insights into familiarity with each ignition system, but knowing the basic differences between the two was far from the acquisition of "second nature behavior." My experiences prompted me to be vigilant for any number of habits born of handling a flintlock in the field, as well as those that focused on maintenance at home, in camp, and in the woods.

Initially, I thought the only realistic way to gain that behavior, was to *learn-by-doing* aka "experiential learning." Essentially, use the gun every day and try to distill knowledge by experimenting with different modern lubes, patching, powder charges and rearranging the loading components upon my person and in my shooting bag.

By trial and error, maybe I would be able to obtain muscle memory and skill by active experimentation and incrementally modifying my approach. However, therein laid the problem; those efforts were based upon my *contemporary* methods and materials.

Regardless of my dedication, I remained ignorant of the *historic* methods and materials. It took me some years to learn that the natural behavior I sought, as a neophyte to

The Conversion Begins

flintlock muzzleloaders, was not going to be found in the use of modern day crutches. Rather, experiential learning in this instance without a proper historical premise was like trying to learn in a vacuum.

My initial pursuit at the time had simply been focused on mastering the flintlock, but what I continued to run into were dozens of questions such as:

-How did the common soldier or militiaman protect his firearm and priming powder from the elements?

-What precautions were taken by a colonial farmer in Virginia, to maintain his flintlock long gun that accompanied him to the field every day?

-What accoutrements did the average shooter, hunter, farmer take into the woods to maintain his flintlock?

I would continue to be challenged by these questions and many more until I realized the relevance and interpretation of the very artifacts from that time which were used to service flintlocks. Another facet I had been overlooking was the study of historical references in early writings, namely: logs, ledgers, diaries and receipts.

In time I came across the image of a "lock cover" [14] in my **Longhunter Sketchbook** by author, Dr. James A. Hanson. I also stumbled into an article about these covers in Mark A. Baker's column, *A Pilgrim's Journey,* appearing in a 1986 issue of **Muzzleloader Magazine** [15] which had been sitting on my shelf from the year before. In order to determine whether these covers worked, I quickly drafted a pattern that would fit my rifle. I located a good piece of dark-brown deer hide, and after I measured and cut the deer hide according to my pattern, I sewed up a lock cover. I then dressed it with a goodly portion of mink oil to repel the moisture. Now I was eager to go out, in the very rain, sleet and snow I had tried to avoid in the past, and test my new creation.

After only a handful of opportunities to use the lock cover in varying types of precipitation I concluded it worked quite well for a number of reasons. Firstly, it kept the lock area dry and it was correct for the time period of my rifle. Secondly, I found the soft deer skin cover to be quiet and it removed easily and quickly. Thirdly, it could be deployed simply by tying it on over the lock area. After being tied on, it could be pulled over the lock or back from it. It was quick to replace after reloading versus the use of Vaseline or wax which, after the shot, would have to be reapplied in order to protect the lock area. I recalled having watched others use Vaseline and candle wax with some limited success.

Clearly, those substances made a mess in an area where a shooter does not want any impediments like chunks of wax or globs of goo to contend with after each shot.

Lastly, when I had seen others use a plastic bag to cover the lock, I observed that it was loud and became brittle in the cold. Plastic was also easily torn by twigs and thorns leaving an open gash into which water and snow could freely penetrate. Buckskin, on the other hand, was durable in any temperature. The buckskin lock cover has been a part of my shooting pouch ever since.

Researching, making and using the lock cover reinforced the basic lesson that, experiential learning of historical skills would be successful only by following hands-on *historical methods*. Up to that point, I had not been able to solve the idiosyncrasies of an 18th century flintlock by using 20th century thinking, no matter how clever. Narrowing my efforts to work within the parameters of historic life ways, materials, and tools commonly used *in the*

The Conversion Begins

age of the flintlock, actually opened my mind to the answers I had been fumbling to find.

In retrospect, I felt somewhat like a blood hound discerning some scent here and there, determined to track down the answers to the very mysteries that, only a few years before, had seemed like a cold forgotten trail, shrouded in the fog of time.

Further, my continued efforts would only bear fruit *if* I avoided the tendency to resort back to the crutches of the Twentieth Century. I was not, after all, just converting a caplock to a flintlock, I was also converting my whole way of thinking. I could finally see that my progress had been hindered until after I had removed my arrogant insistence and stubborn dependence on modern methodologies, and replaced them with historical methodologies.

The Conversion Begins

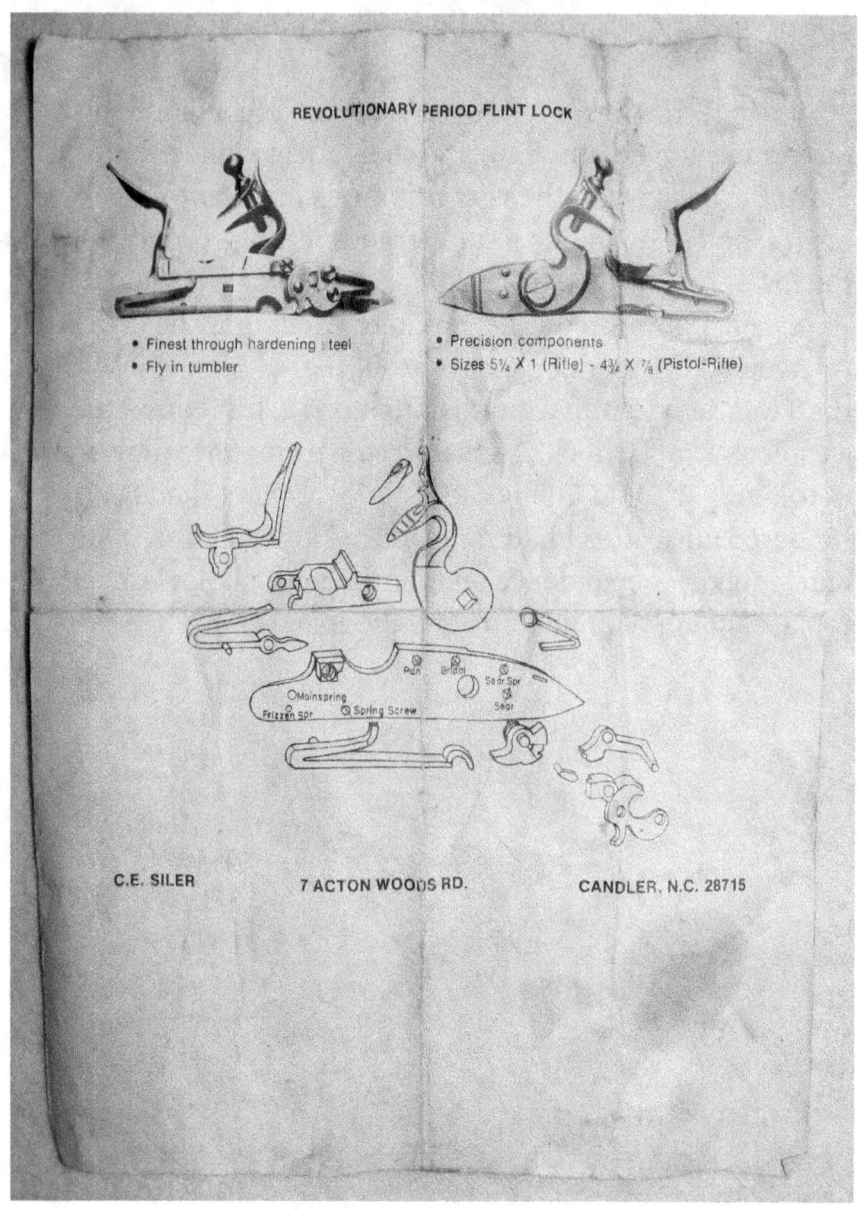

The reverse side of the lock assembly directions for the Siler Flintlock showing inside and outsside of the lock and the exploded view. Copyright C.E. Siler, rights acquired by Jim Chambers

My Journey with Deerfoot

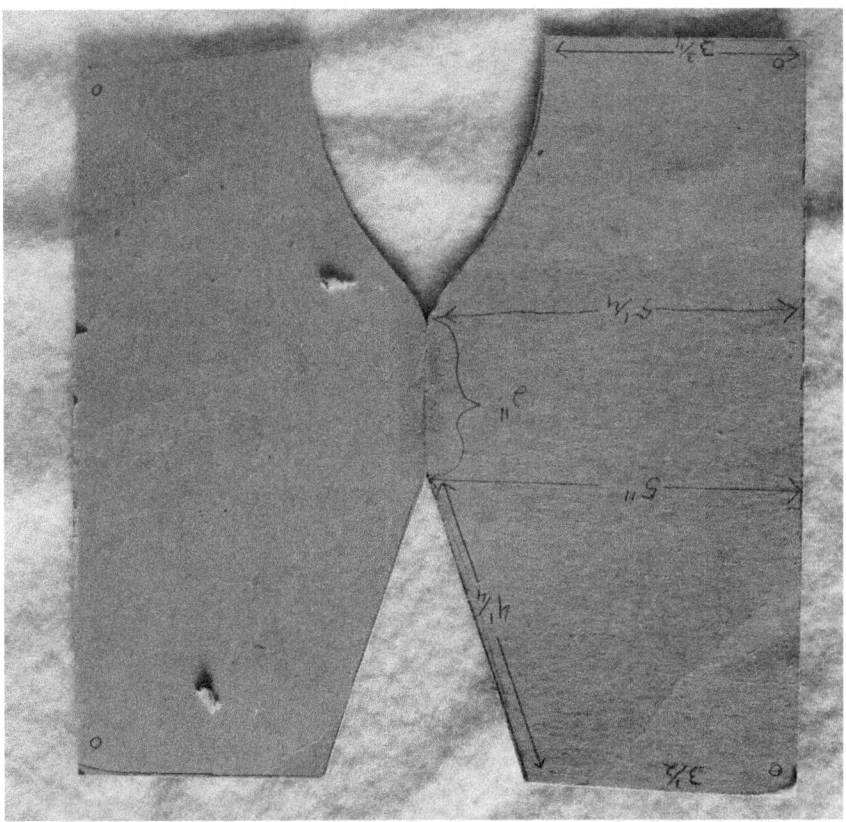

This is the basic one piece pattern for my lock cover made from cardboard. It is 10-1/2" long; 3-1/3" inches tall at the front and back, and 5" to 5-1/4" in the middle. Each side of the front "V" is 4-1/4 inches long, the rear slightly longer.
The top of the photo, is the front of the cover, it reaches over the barrel. The bottom of the photo is the back of the cover, it reaches over the wrist. Use medium weight deer skin,
Start at the point of each "V" and sew each shut using a plain-welted seam to form a small tent. (A welted seam uses a welt in between the two sides, the edges of each side are visible as is an edge of the welt.) The finished seam appears on the outside of the cover. The un-cut 2" portion in the middle fits over the cock (on half-cock) and frizzen (closed).
At the corners (marked with circles), attach thongs 15" to 18" long. These should also be of deer skin. When assembly is complete, dress with several applications of mink oil, deer tallow or a pine tar based dressing like Hubbards shoe grease.

The Conversion Begins

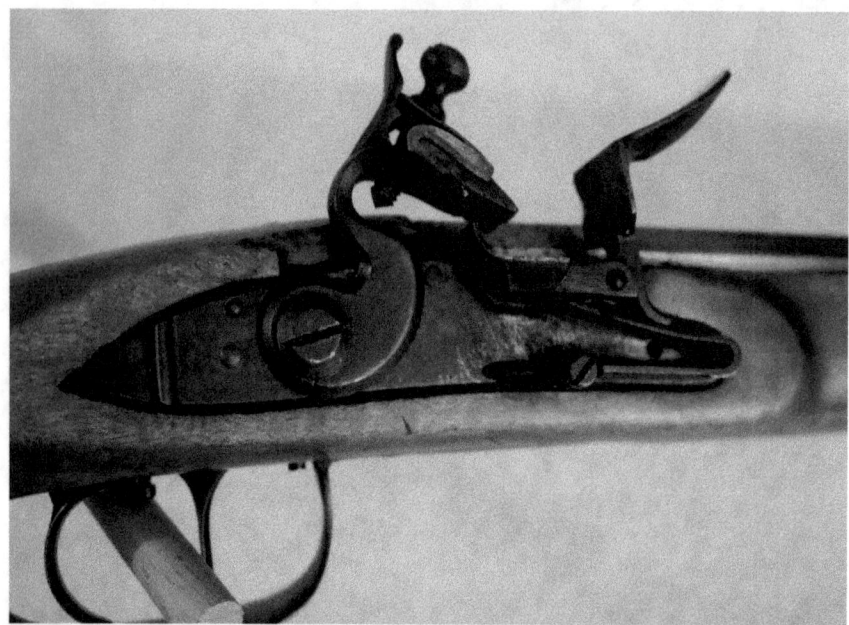

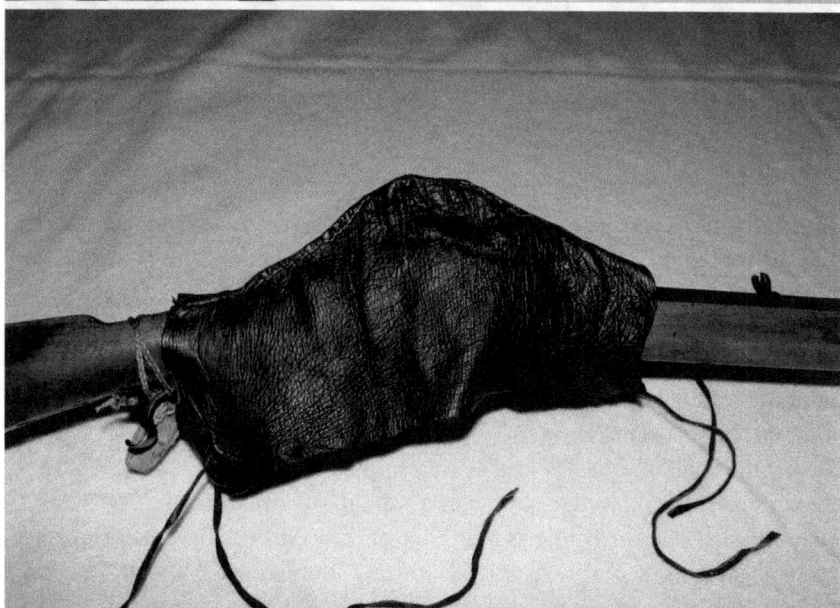

Top-The completed Siler small-rifle lock fitting perfectly into the lock mortise, ready to spark.
Bottom-The lock cover of deer skin, heavily oiled to resist precipitation. This is tied down to the stock; fore and aft of the lock area and even covers the triggers.

Top-Author at the Rapid River Rendezvous with Deerfoot, August 1987. Notice the cloth shirt, the leather shirt had been shelved by this time.
Bottom-A haul of squirrels on the canoe. The shooting bag that started out servicing the T/C Hawken now converted for Deerfoot. Notice the second horn with finer powder, a practice which the author later found unnecessary.

Chapter 5
Three Diversions *or rather* Stepping Stones

Looking in hindsight on the well-marked road, which today appears so inevitable, it was anything but a sure path in the years before I walked its length. -Author-

My desire to acquire proficiency with flintlocks was becoming an obsession. The more I dwelt on the subject, the more I could envision owning several such firearms whether rifle, smoothbore or pistol. However, the path in between my own mile-markers of "success" was hardly a straight one.

In reality, I was not quite ready to let go of my use of caplocks. Just as attractive at that time, was the prospect of versatility, whether the gun was flintlock or caplock. Though flint would be more desirable, I opted for several diversions. I would gladly take the concession of another caplock when cost and convenience became a factor, but eventually, I would bring all my muzzleloaders into line with the flintlock ethic. First, however, I had to let the "obsession with versatility" run its course.

Diversion 1. The Heaviest Concession

My early efforts to diversify, in 1986, were based upon using the T/C as the platform for a back-up rifle. I thought I might like to start with a thirty-two inch, interchangeable Green Mountain barrel in .45 caliber. It was one inch across the flats and made to fit the T/C stock with a hook end breech. Putting the new barrel on the stock required little effort. I removed the ramrod and wedge key, hinged the .54 barrel up and out and in its place inserted the "hook-end," of the breech on the Green Mountain barrel, into the tang.

Three Diversions/Stepping Stones

I then hinged it down into the barrel channel, followed by replacing wedge key. The barrel also came with a thirty-two inch polymer ramrod and a threaded brass fitting for attaching jags. Now I had two rifles of the same caliber.

One of my intentions was to try it as a heavy 'brush buster" and in that vein, picked up a box of .45 caliber conical bullets from the Buffalo Bullet Company. These solid based conical projectiles, often called "buffalo bullets," were made of 325 grains of soft lead. As far as conical bullets go they were good for mushrooming and carried a lot of foot pounds at longer distances.

The problem with my approach was the Green Mountain barrel had a 1:66 rate of twist and cut with .010 of an inch deep rifling for use with round balls, not *conicals*. The barrel was a tack driver with round balls, but the twist was too slow to stabilize the heavy conicals. In order to shoot any conical bullet, the twist needed to be at least 1:40 and the depth of the rifling must be cut no deeper than .005 of an inch.

With my set-up, it required ninety grains of FFg to stabilize the bullet out to thirty or so yards. It was a punishing exercise to shoot the conicals. Also, the barrel was sighted in at forty yards for round balls, which have a lighter mass of only 127 grains. Therefore, if I shot the conicals, I had to improvise by changing my sight picture. The bullets would usually stabilize out to fifty yards, but out past that they would often "key-hole," that is to say, impact the target sideways.

At that point I gave up any thought of using it with conicals and instead loaded it with round balls. As long as it had it, I might as well use it.

With two guns in my possession, I brought it to

the stand about five or six times, but it soon became more trouble than it was worth. It was pretty heavy and I had to make sure I had a capper with percussion caps. I also kept it behind the seat of my truck during the muzzleloader deer season where it was ready for action, but saw little, if any, action. I used that particular barrel for about two years. During which time I shot some squirrels, grouse, rabbits, porcupines (but never a deer). Otherwise, it sat in the closet.

Every time I opted to use it instead of Deerfoot, I felt as though I was missing an opportunity to gain more experience with a flintlock. That feeling seemed to lessen my enjoyment of muzzleloading. I would not "step off of that stone" until I sold the barrel in a trade.

Diversion 2. A Lighter Concession

In the Winter of 1986-87, not long after I had purchased the Green Mountain barrel, a much more streamlined approach came to mind as I considered a pistol. While I was at Track of the Wolf, I looked through the bargain-bin and came across a pistol half-stock which was 98% inlet and well coated in varnish. Also available were some trigger guards, triggers and ramrod pipes specifically for that stock.

I believe I paid twelve dollars for the stock, three dollars each for the trigger guards, two dollars each for the triggers and several dollars for the ramrod pipes. I was happy to get the parts and the store was happy to clear a small portion of its old, discontinued inventory. However, there was no lock to fit the pistol stock in their inventory. The problem would have to be solved by contacting Numerich Arms Company in New York in order to obtain a caplock to fit. The process could take about six weeks and roughly twenty-eight dollars plus shipping.

Three Diversions/Stepping Stones

I called Numerich Arms and had an informative conversation with the representative. He told me to take a look at another place in Minneapolis, called Muzzleloaders Et Cetera which may have several of the sought after locks. If the store did not have a lock, I could order one from Numerich.

Several weeks later, while visiting in the Twin Cities area, I headed over to Lyndale Avenue and located the shop. I found they had three locks in stock, but I only bought one. Perhaps I should have bought them all, but I had limited funds. It was a European lock with a tightly pinched main spring which, if it broke, had no source of ready replacements, except to have one custom made to fit.

All I wanted at that time was a lock that fit the mortise in the stock, so I was willing to risk the broken spring contingency.

Once I had all the parts I contacted Gene Shadley for some assistance. We worked out a trade and he assembled the pistol. I had also been asking about belt hooks and, lo and behold, Gene just happened to have a belt hook and installed it.

Now I had a pistol in the same caliber as my rifle, that was ready to be taken into the field. It was a solid, accurate piece which ended up accompanying me on a number of squirrel hunting forays as well as fall canoe trips. It would also come in handy on a deer drive, only it would be in another's hands, not mine. I would not "step off of that stone" until I sold it and replaced it with a flintlock pistol.

Diversion 3. A Platform of Convenience

Not quite a year passed after my purchase of the .45 caliber Green Mountain barrel before I toyed with another application for my Thompson/Center stock. Maybe I could fit it with a Twenty gauge smooth bore barrel. At the time, Montana Barrel Company, had been closed, but in its place had opened Bausca Barrel Company. In June 1987 I contacted them, and after about two months and a few phone calls, I obtained a Thirty-six inch long, one inch-barrel with a 20 gauge bore and threaded at the breech for a T/C breech plug, for about $70.00 plus shipping.

I had never owned a shotgun or smooth bore muzzleloader so I was eager to continue the diversification of the my T/C "Hawken" stock as a platform for either a rifle or a smoothbore.

In this case all I needed was a breech plug with an integral bolster for the barrel, that would fit over the T/C lock. In Late August 1987, with a good deal of importuning, I convinced one of the gun workers at Track to remove the breech plug from an older T/C barrel. Several weeks later, I enlisted the help of a gunsmith who installed the breech plug on the barrel.

With the barrel back in my hands, I filed a dove-tail into the bottom flats of the barrel to accept the loop for the wedge key that held the barrel onto the stock. Following that I would have to get a custom-length under rib installed on the barrel in order to attach the ramrod pipes for a longer ramrod. The T/C was a half-stock so the under rib was necessary to create a surface 3/8" from the bottom of the barrel, to install the pipes. Without the under rib, the pipes would not line up with the ramrod hole in the stock. The whole process took several more weeks while I was waiting on parts or the availability of shop time.

I wanted to shoot it, and hunt with it so instead of being deterred, I used electrical tape to temporarily attach the under rib as well as the ramrod pipes. Lastly, I inserted a percussion nipple into the breech bolster and I was in business just in time for a weekend hunting trip with Little Crow.

Several weeks later I was able to have both the under rib and ramrod pipes attached correctly and permanently and thus, my project was complete.

With my relatively small outlay of cash, I too could now compete with other folks shooting clays with shotguns and trade guns. I continued to practice with it for use on birds, but it was a chore to swing as the stock did not have nearly enough drop to make sighting down the barrel comfortable. It was, however, a dependable caplock muzzleloader that allowed me to experience shooting birds with shot.

Since I did not have a pouch just for bird shot, I took a day to make one which would hold a couple of pounds of shot. At first I put a wooden plug in the top of the all-leather spout to keep the shot inside. The spout, however would fold over and impede the flow of shot and I knew I would have to redesign the opening. For the time being, though, I had a "shot pouch" and it allowed me to pour out a known volume of shot using my powder measure.

A month later I remedied the pouch problem by inserting a section of copper pipe which made the spout stiff. Following that, I made a stopper of a smaller diameter of copper pipe and inserted a wooden plug with a knob at one end for a shot measure. In order to achieve a friction fit for my new measure/stopper, I wrapped a small sheet of cork around it and glued it in place, (looking back the better option would have been to sew a layer of deer skin around the pipe).

My Journey with Deerfoot

I made an attractive skinny braided strap out of leather lace which I would quickly learn was too small and cut into my shoulder; even if the pouch was only half-full of shot. Regardless of the limitations of the strap, the pouch was ready for use in the upcoming fall hunting season.

With the advent of the canoe trip the following autumn, (1988) on the Bigfork River, I was torn whether to take my flintlock rifle or my new 20 ga caplock. The deciding factor was the prevalence of grouse in that area and almost no gray squirrels, therefore, I decided to go with my caplock. Several hours into our float, on Saturday morning, my friend, Joe "Swamper" Wirtz and I found ourselves combing through the hazel patches along the river with good success.

The hunt itself was fun, if not comical as the two of us could not seem to walk twenty yards without a grouse popping up, begging to be shot. We kept abreast of each other as we paralleled the river. In a short distance, I shot a bird as did Swamper. I had no sooner loaded when Swamper asked if he could use my gun, because he had another bird in the thick brush. He had not loaded is own gun yet and did not want to lose sight of the bird. Therefore, he had me hold his .50 caliber rifle "Dancing Bears," and gave me some .490 balls and I reloaded and capped it as he slipped off after that bird.

Again, I had no sooner reloaded Swamper's rifle, when I spied a grouse that I shot in the neck. I had just finished re-loading his rifle, yet again, when I heard Swamper shoot his second bird in the dense brush.

We came together and handed-off guns once more. I quickly reloaded mine and continued to keep moving through the hazel. Soon, Swamper shot at another bird and it spooked my way, which I shot as soon as it landed.

Three Diversions/Stepping Stones

Then after reloading Swamper was close enough to whisper a request to use my gun again, so we came together and traded guns. He slipped off to the edge of a swamp and took another grouse. As he was heading back I spied a grouse and shot at it, but since I could not reload, I waited for him to return. Upon meeting, we both reloaded our respective guns and headed toward the shot bird. We had not walked another ten yards before he shot at a bird and missed. He had me stop until he could reload and it was then we both realized he had clipped it. As it came running my way I also clipped it in the leg and it was now half hopping and half flying in the thick brush. We both zeroed in on a stump behind which it was hiding. As soon as I had eyes on the bird, I told him I was close enough for a shot. When I pulled the trigger I was about eight yards away and completely took off the bird's head.

As I was reloading, Swamper picked up the bird and jokingly said, "Yeah, I'd say you were close enough."

The rest of the party who had been waiting at the canoes came to see the reason for all the shooting. They conferred amongst themselves that we must have had a porcupine stuck high-up in a tree, and were trying to shoot the branch out from underneath it. Upon seeing all the grouse we were carrying, they asked why we did not tell them. Our reply was, *"we did not dare leave the birds; because they were right in front of us, ready to shoot."* Swamper and I had to chuckle as we nodded at each other.

No one could argue with the fact that we had taken a considerable number of birds. I measured our canoe trip as a great success due to the blessings of our hunt. Even though I had taken more grouse with a muzzleloader in that day than I had on any other day prior to that, I felt like I was missing something. A part of me wished that I had taken all those birds with a flintlock. Though I had decided to take that firearm prior to the canoe trip, it had not been a hands-down choice. I felt like I was somehow shorting myself by not having Deerfoot with me. I could only wonder whether a flintlock rifle in my hand would have yielded as many birds, but even that was not the most relevant assessment. Rather, the crux of the matter was I wanted to rely on a flintlock for all my hunting needs. In the end I had to admit that I just did not have the same fulfillment with a caplock as I did with a flintlock. Nothing against caplocks, but that is how I felt.

    For almost two years, it was fun to have a type of "shotgun" in my repertoire which gave me the flexibility to go hunting with a rifle or a smoothbore. As I look back and consider all the idiosyncracies of the 20 ga barrel on that T/C stock, it was only preparing me for the welcomed ergonomics of a historically styled fowler. As is often the case, I would need to struggle a little while longer with that barrel/stock set-up, until I was ready to give it up and replace it. I would not "step off of this third stone" until I traded the barrel for some gunsmithing.

    Though these diversions, gave me insight into other muzzleloading applications, they were not the final destination. Yes, I had learned from them, but it was time to move on and admit I was trying to hold on to old baggage, like stones in a bag. Finally, the realization came to me, that having a diverse array of muzzleloaders, did not mean nearly as much as gaining more experience with one or two flintlocks. If I continued to rely on caplocks like old baggage, they would simply weigh me down. In treating them like stones, it was best to let go of them, leave them and recognize they were a part of the path that now lay behind me.

Chapter 6
Molded by Tradition

A note of caution, *due to harmful vapors, melting and pouring molten lead should only be performed in a well ventilated area or outdoors!*

During the winter of 1987-1988, I came across six pounds or so of soft lead (no tin or antimony) and thought I could use it to make ammunition. Possession of the lead provoked me to investigate casting my own round balls. It seemed like a cheaper and definitely a more self-reliant approach to muzzleloading.

In one of my stops at Track, before heading up to the cabin, I noticed that loading blocks, replete with spru-cutter, were on sale; just what I needed for my endeavor. I purchased a set of blocks, with double cavities for .440 round balls; as well as the handles necessary to hold and operate the blocks. To melt the lead, I purchased a small, four ounce sheet-iron pot sporting a bail that I could use over the fire.

When I arrived at the cabin, late Friday evening, my first duty was to get the fire going in the barrel stove. As the fire slowly grew, I could see a good bed of coals building up so I took advantage of them. I placed some pieces of lead in the small pot and using a long set of pliers, steadily placed the pot on the coals. In a few minutes I had molten lead. With gloved hands and long sleeves, I carefully pulled the small pot out of the stove with my right hand. In my left hand I held the handles of the new mold and rested the blocks upon the cement floor and began pouring the molten lead into the two cavities. I tried to reduce the amount of spillage when filling the molds, but as each over-pour occurred I let the blobs harden. I quickly grabbed the still-hot blobs with a pliers and put them back into the melting pot.

The first several pours resulted in wrinkled balls, which is a sign that the mold is too cold. Not long after however, I began to achieve smooth, round balls with a shiny, mirror-finish. They were perfect.

As the night wore on I concentrated on getting at least fifty round balls for my use. When I had finally achieved at least fifty good balls, I pulled the pot out to cool, but not before accidentally dumping part of the lead into the cinders. For that clean-up I would have to wait until the next morning to locate the "ingot" of lead and pull it out before stoking up the fire for the day.

The next morning I found the ingot, I cut it up and placed the pieces back into the pot to melt. When it was finally molten, I fluxed it with beeswax to clean it. After the beeswax was stirred into the molten metal, the dross, impurities in the form of wood ash, came to the surface. I strained it out with an old stainless-steel tea spoon which I had salvaged from a rummage pile. Following that, I made about twenty more balls.

That day I considered a more refined approach to the making of round balls by using an electric production pot, which several of my friends owned. By doing so, I could avoid so much spillage when filling the mold. Though I would continue to mold round balls at the occasional camp fire, I also made up my mind not do so until I had an actual lead ladle for the purpose of pouring the molten lead into the mold, instead of tilting the little four ounce pot itself.

Just the same, I felt a sense of achievement, as though I had earned another badge for self-sufficiency. I still had a lot to learn in my efforts to run ball, but it was a good start.

Over the next five years I would go on to mold several thousand balls with that particular ball mold. The steel held up well and continues, to this day, to mold good balls. I keep it greased in order to prevent rusting inside the cavities, which in turn keeps the inside smooth.

Although I enjoyed using the mold, it was heavy and bulky and certainly not anything I would bring with me to a camp. From the time I obtained the mold, it stayed at home.

A Mold for the Shooting Bag

I ended up ordering my first bag mold from Rapine Bullet Mold Co. Inc. At the time, they were doing a brisk business in all sorts of bullet molds, but especially ball molds which they marketed as "bag moulds." This mold was used to cast balls to use in a fowling piece referenced in chapter 7.

I continued to learn about molds and their uses starting with the bag mold which is a simple lighter design. It opens and closes no differently than a basic pair of pliers. The lead is poured into the concave sprue hole between the blocks. However, it does not have a rotating cutter, rather the sprue cutter is behind the jaws in the forward-most part of the handles, otherwise, the process is relatively the same. When pouring into the sprue hole, however the lead must be allowed to "bead-up" on top of the mold. The lead hardens a few seconds later and, when removed from the cavity, the bead on top resembles a mushroom protruding from the ball.

The easiest way to remove the solid (but still hot) ball from the mold is by using a set of pliers to clamp onto the mushroom-portion of the sprue. Once the mold is opened up, the ball is gently dislodged from one side or other of the mold cavity. Just because the lead is solidified, does not mean it can be touched; it remains hot for some time and can cause a nasty burn. Caution dictates wearing gloves during the molding process. Once the lead is cool enough to touch with the bare hand, the sprues can be cut off with the sprue cutter on the mold handles or a pair of plain tin-snips can be used for the operation.

Also, DO NOT cool down the mold blocks or the lead with water! This is a ruinous effort that will warp the mold blocks, and can make the round ball misshapen.

For the best results the blocks need to stay hot. A properly heated mold will cast shiny balls. But if it becomes too hot, the balls will develop a "glazed" or "frosted" look somewhat like dull aluminum. When that develops, the mold should be allowed to cool a while.

When the mold is too cool it will cast wrinkled balls. Generally, by casting two or three balls and allowing the lead to stay in the mold for a half a minute before removing it, the mold will heat up sufficiently. The wrinkled balls should be put back into the lead pot to remelt while they are still hot.

At one point I tried several pounds of wheel weights which, though they were free, contained too much antimony to yield a soft lead round ball. The balls molded with these weights, being harder and lighter in weight, patterned differently. They lack malleability and resist obduration.

The key advantage of using soft lead is its malleability. Upon hitting a deer or other large game animal, the projectile should expand. Soft lead can flatten out to as much as double its original size, which will, in turn, enlarge the wound channel. Balls cast with antimony, however, will not deform or expand.

As a quick test, your "thumb-nail" should cut into the surface and leave a shiny track. If the nail skips off, it is too hard and should not be used in a muzzleloader. Balls recovered after being shot should retain thread impressions from the weaving in the cloth patching.

Molded by Tradition

Top-Palmetto blocks with double .440 cavities. The attached handles clamp the blocks together. The sprue cutter, which is pivoted forward in this image, is rotated a quarter turn clockwise to position the holes over the cavities and is ready to pour. After the poured lead hardens, the long lobe is struck forward to cut the sprues. This set of molds stay in the shop as they are heavy and bulky.
Bottom-The hot pot used to melt lead over a heat source, 3" in diameter x 2" high. This pot is stored in the shooting box, ready to use in camps if ammunition runs low.

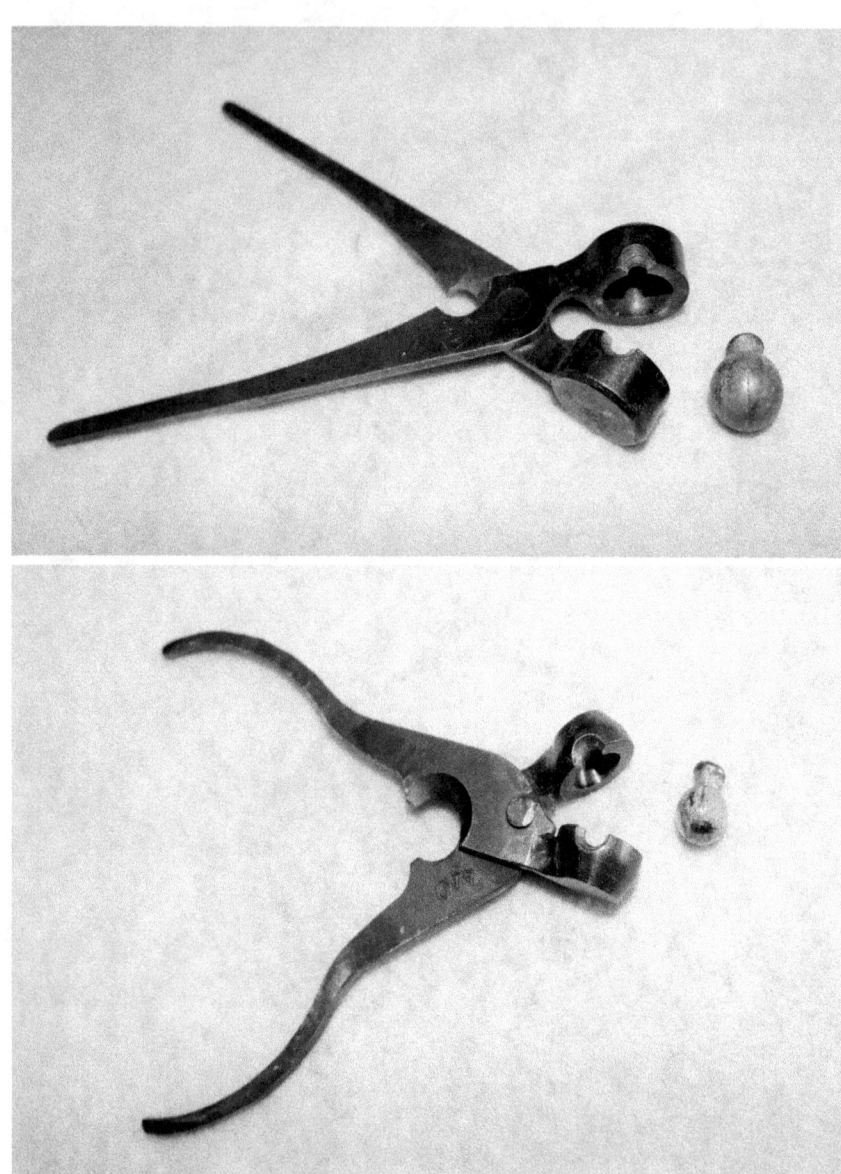

Top-The earlier straight-handled Rapine ball mold for my 12 ga fowling piece. Bottom-A "bag-mold" made for .440. Purchased from Larry Callahan in 2014. This mold stays in the shooting bag and is used in camps or on the trail. A round ball is kept in the mold to prevent the blocks from raking or twisting off-center. Notice each ball has its distinctive mushroom after molding. It can be cut off using the circular nippers in the crotch of the handles.

Chapter 7
My Expanding Efforts with Flintlocks

In the following spring of 1988, I looked forward to the events and gatherings of summer as well as a new project. While at Track, I came across another Italian made .45 caliber barrel for $10.00. Since I already had a trigger guard and trigger to go with it, all I really needed was a breech plug, a set of ramrod pipes and a side plate. In the week following I also ordered through the mail a maple pistol stock from Pecatonica River Longrifle Supply. This next pistol however would be a flintlock. Not long after I received the stock for the new pistol in the mail, I traded the heavy, one-inch, .45 caliber, caplock barrel to defray the cost of the last necessary component, a new Small Siler flintlock, identical to the one used in Deerfoot. For the second time in my muzzleloading career, I had committed my efforts towards shooting a flintlock instead of a caplock.

    I took the time to inlet the barrel into the stock and then handed it over to Gene Shadley who, thank goodness, masterfully inlet the lock, along with the trigger guard and ramrod pipes.

    After concluding terms of payment, I received the pistol, "in-the-white." [16] I finished the wood using aqua fortis[17] and linseed oil which brought out the grain and curl nicely. Thus accoutered, I could take both rifle and pistol into the brush or the deer-stand, use the same ammunition, prime both with powder and freed myself from dependence on percussion caps. It was a perfect match and I was determined to use the "duo" as often as possible.

    During that same time, I signed on to work at the Forest History Center near Grand Rapids, MN. My supervisor, Skip Drake, schooled me in the art of being a professional, historical interpreter at the circa 1900 logging camp. This was a great opportunity to take part in experiential learning whether it be cutting wood with a two-man cross-cut saw, sharpening those saws, blacksmithing, leather repair as well as handling horses.

It came at the perfect time. Not only was I seeking experience in the use of an earlier ignition system at home, I was also employed in a historical setting within which I could gain the knowledge of skills that had remained virtually unaltered since the eighteenth century.

During my on-duty hours, I observed, Bill Carpenter, deftly work iron on a coal forge, where in his spare time, he made a pair of pliers. When I asked about his willingness to make another pair for purchase, he not only agreed to make them, but arranged several opportunities for me to sit-in while he crafted the new set from scratch. I still have them to this day.

Here was the perfect opportunity to obtain iron tools and hooks which were forged on the spot; the very thing a colonial man would encounter. From time to time, I purchased or traded with Bill for any number of items, but it did not stop there.

Curious, I inquired whether he could weld several chain-saw files together in a twist pattern to make a "C" shaped striker for me. He said he would like to try and bade me give to him six worn-out saw files, just for good measure. The next day he set to work on several strikers and two days later he presented me with my own striker that looked like a segmented worm. Best of all the new striker threw a good shower of sparks.

At the next rendezvous I used the striker in a fire

Expanding My Efforts with Flintlocks

starting contest which allowed me to claim a first place. It still continues to throw good sparks to this day.

At that same time I watched as Bill crafted a belt hook for a pistol, which he decorated with the chisel to resemble a balsam branch. I ended up purchasing that hook and then set about to forge my own.

When I had time off the following week, I used the blacksmith shop to forge a belt hook from a 3/8" bolt, which I eventually installed on the flintlock pistol. The addition of a hook eased my ability to carry the pistol in a handy position on my belt.

Even though I usually worked Saturdays or Sundays, I rarely worked both days. As summer wore on, I was able to attend three more rendezvous, though for two of them I had only one day of attendance. By early September, I managed one more rendezvous at which I shot as much as possible.

I endeavored to use up my commercial round balls so I could replace them with my own home-molded ones. I shot with Deerfoot and my new flintlock pistol all weekend long.

Most of the targets required five shots for score and there were at least five to six targets for rifle and two for pistol. In addition to the paper targets there were, it seemed, an endless number of novelty targets such as: crossed-straws, feather quills, pigeon-in-the-hole, charcoal on strings, poker chips on strings and dominoes on a strings, split-the-round ball (on an ax edge), tiny cloth bags of flour, and on and on. The targets were only limited by the range officer's imagination. My numerous summer shooting activities allowed me to hone my skills for small game season, and hopefully a successful deer season.

After the start of my third year of school, I tried to get up to the cabin as much as possible prepared to hunt. I generally arrived at eight to nine o'clock Friday evening and the following dawn generally found me quietly slipping into the tall woods, equipped with both rifle and pistol in search of bushytails, rabbits and grouse. On several of the long three day weekends, I recall bagging three to five squirrels before noon on each day. Though I could have hunted every weekend clear to the end of October, I still needed to focus on my studies, so I would not be out in the woods again until Muzzleloader deer season in late November.

With the arrival of 1988 muzzleloader deer season I had one three-day weekend away from school to connect with a deer and return to study for final exams. I was earnestly looked forward to getting out and hopefully shooting a deer. Perhaps this would be the year marked by success with my flintlock.

During that season I recall a drive by three of us with Swamper sitting in a tree. I could see several deer on the edge of the woods, but they were more than one hundred yards away. Then I saw him shoot from across the open logging slash and shortly thereafter he shot again.

I thought, *How in the world could Swamper have reloaded and shot within twenty seconds?* My answer came after the drive, when we all assembled. I learned that he had used *my* .45 caliber caplock pistol.

Swamper related, upon exiting his car, he saw my pistol case and in it my pistol. Since it would be of no use sitting there, brought it with him to the stand. After shooting the doe, he used the pistol to take the rather large fawn as well, hence the quick, second shot.

Well, I had not taken a deer, but one of my pistols did. Further, if I had not brought the pistol in the first place, the second deer would have gotten away. I guess it was some consolation, but it did not change the fact that I could not seem to connect with a deer that year. Deerfoot was with me the whole time I sought to take a deer, but I did not shoot it. It was becoming a worn-out story.

Sad to say, that year only afforded me with a few fleeting opportunities of seeing deer off in the distance. The season came to a close without firing a shot or even putting my sights on a deer. After being out in the woods for three days, I headed back to St. Paul to concentrate on school. With disappointment staring me in the face, I had to concede my failure and wait for next year…again.

Yet Another Flinter

In early 1989 I had the opportunity to acquire a Harrington and Richards 12 gauge shotgun barrel. It was not yet machined at the breech to accept shells. Rather, it was a smooth tube, thick at the breech and trimmed down at the muzzle, cylinder bore. It needed only to be tapped at the breech to accept a breech plug. At about that same time, I sold my percussion pistol and used the money to make my next purchase of a fowler style maple stock. I kept the new, smooth barrel and fowler stock stored until I had the opportunity to acquire the rest of the parts.

Late in 1989, I finally purchased a round faced English-style Tryon flintlock, made by Davis Lock company, along with a butt plate, trigger guard for a fowler, ramrod pipes and other furniture; all iron. I saw no reason to deviate from the use of all-iron mountings. My thinking had been that just as Deerfoot was iron mounted, this would work for the fowler as well.

In April 1990, I handed the whole works off to Gene Shadley who worked on it though the Spring and into the

Summer. By early June he had finished assembling my English fowler. It was a joy to shoulder and I could sight down the barrel with ease. I still had more work to do on the fowler, but it was operational and solidly built.

I disassembled the fowler, darkened the stock with aqua fortis, and finished it with linseed oil. I also browned the barrel and iron furniture. After re-assembling the fowler, I spent time on patterning it for shot. I did not have a supply of round balls, but I had acquired several different sizes to compare their performance and ease of loading. At that time I used patched round balls (long before I learned about "double-wadding) and the heavier the patch I used with a smaller ball, the more accurate my shots tended to be.

Since I could not find a reliable source of round balls to fit the .730 inside diameter of the barrel, I considered the purchase of another ball mold. It just so happened several months earlier, at a local rendezvous, I had received a catalog for the Rapine Bullet Mold Co., which offered many choices in conical bullet and ball molds.

The style I chose, named after the English fashion as a "bag mould," resembled those made in the eighteenth century (see p. 84). It was light enough carry in the shooting bag and produced a .685 ball. After molding several dozen balls with it, I tried moderately thick canvas for patching which produced the most consistent results.

Four months later, I exchanged the 20 gauge barrel, used on the T/C stock, for some gunsmithing work. It had served its purpose, but it was merely a stepping stone as I continued to advance all my shooting activities to flintlock ignitions.

I now had three flintlocks: Deerfoot the rifle, the Kentucky styled pistol and a smooth bore English fowler.

Expanding My Efforts with Flintlocks

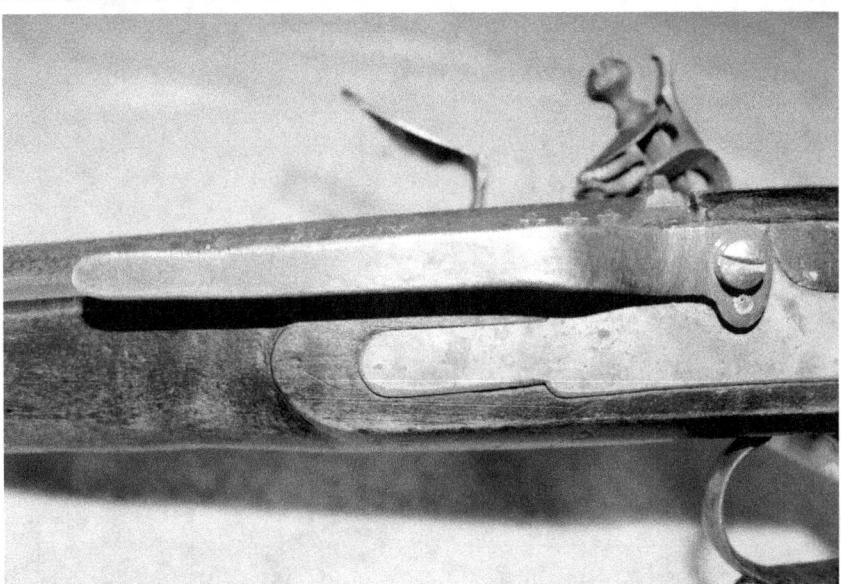

Top-The author's .45 caliber Flintlock pistol fitted with a small Siler lock.

Bottom-reverse side showing the belt hook made from a 3/8" steel bolt, which the author fashioned in the coal forge at the Forest History Center.

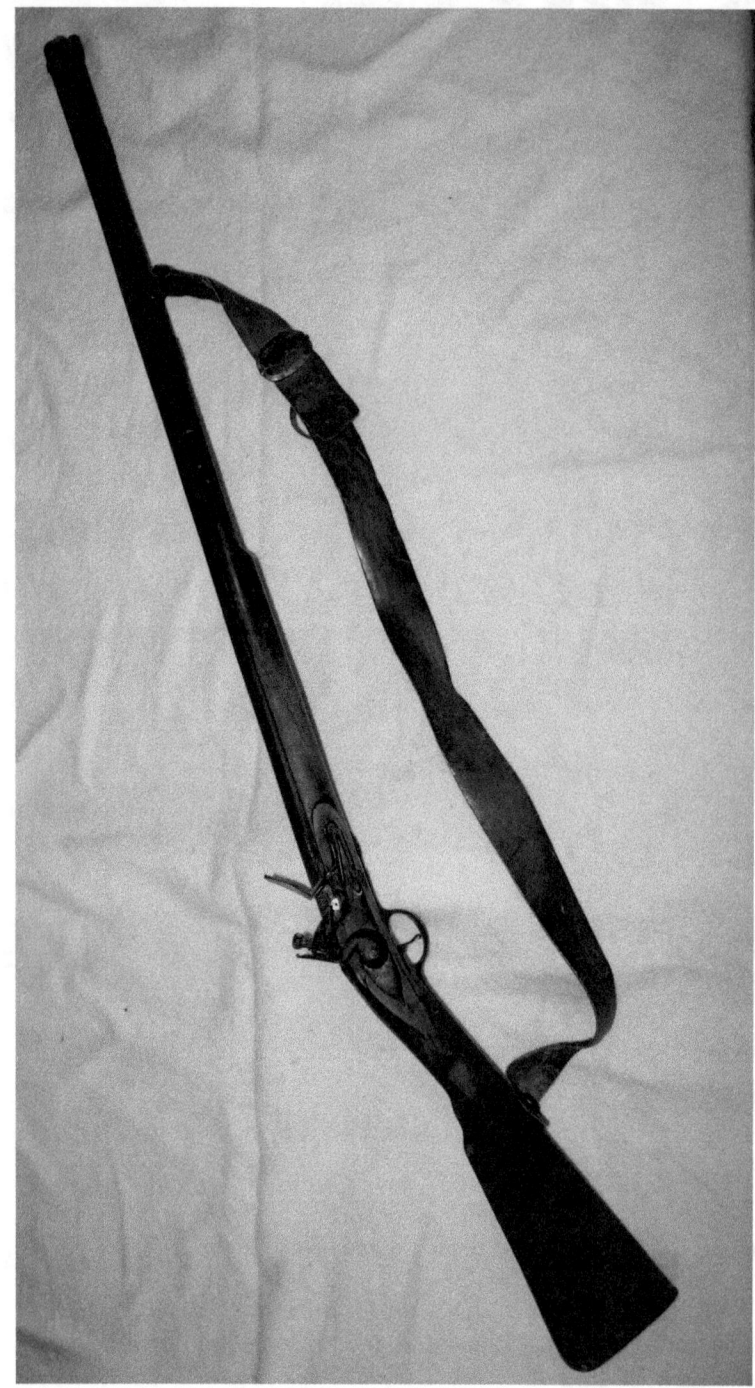

The author's 12 gauge flintlock English fowler. It is iron mounted, there are no brass fittings. Only the buckle on the strap is brass.

Chapter 8
Hard Won Lessons

The following year, 1989, unfolded on a similar basis, but following the advent of graduation, my new endeavor was to study for the bar exam. Though my opportunities to attend camps that summer were significantly curtailed, Deerfoot was with me, leaning in the corner of my bedroom. Its company was enough to remind me that eventually I would be camping at rendezvous and shooting on the line.

After the exam in late July, I attended a rendezvous at Fort Snelling put on by the Minnesota Historical Society. I did not shoot or even bring Deerfoot, as there were plenty of other activities. I camped out under a friend's awning, competed in events, helped cook six buffalo roasts over the fire, and purchased a much needed period correct shirt with some prize money. It was a welcomed reward for my summer efforts, but now I needed some spending money.

Several days later, I headed up to the family farm in Kindred, North Dakota to work the harvest. Deerfoot was packed, of course, and I got to shoot it at some nuisance critters in the farm yard, like woodchucks, as well as some target practice. While I was there, my Uncle George had some scrap iron which he gave to me for a special project.

One of the tools I was lacking was a lead ladle. As I explained my intentions for the piece of steel, my uncle agreed to help by means of his oxy-acetylene torch. He heated the steel to a workable dull-yellow and then I hammered the soft glowing metal over a 1-7/8" trailer hitch. In a mere two heatings we had the bowl shaped with a small spout for pouring. After the third heating, we cut out the stem and with the fourth heating we shaped a tubular handle which would accept a stick. I tried to pay my uncle for his efforts, but he declined and related that he had fun working with the hot steel.

When the grain harvest was done, it was time for plowing. I continued to work the fields for another week after which my Uncle George figured he would take over my chores for the fall maintenance. With that, I headed back to the cabin and before long I was again hunting bushy-tails, hares and grouse amid the vast expanse of Minnesota's northern forests. I was also ready to "run ball" with the newly made ladle.

I began my lead-pouring efforts as before, at the wood stove, and I soon found out, though, that the ladle required heating as much as the hot-pot holding the lead. As long as I kept the ladle hot in the stove, the lead in its bowl stayed molten; if allowed to cool, however, the lead in it would solidify quickly. That meant that I had to have the ladle in the stove almost as much as the hot pot. My compromise was to rest the ladle on the top of the stove, then grab it with gloves when I was ready to use it. I would dip from the hot pot with the ladle and then pour from the ladle into the mold.

The fact that the ladle had a small pour spout did make a difference in directing the stream of lead into the small sprue hole so it was an improvement. The end result was a lot less spilled lead.

Even though I had reduced the spillage, the process was still a bit cumbersome. After several sessions of running ball, however, I began to look for examples of historic ladles to determine how deep the bowl was fashioned. I also wondered how the hunters who were operating far from hearth and home not only melted lead, but how they kept it

Hard Won Lessons

molten while they poured it. Further, I questioned whether the original lead ladles were of a lighter gauge (like sheet metal)? If so, it would be able to take on the heat from the molten lead more quickly.

On a number of occasions I made use of the production pots that my friends had in their shops. It would be a while before I felt more successful with running ball at the camp fire like the woodsmen of old.

I was gratified with my expanding knowledge, skills in muzzleloaders and related equipment, but I still had not taken a deer with a muzzleloader. It was an important facet of my historical interpretation as a longhunter.

Back in the day, hunters like Boone shot lots of deer and sold the hides into the market. I had yet to shoot one with my muzzleloader. I was determined to stick to my goal.

At that time, we muzzleloading hunters were relegated to a few small areas where we could pursue deer in the muzzleloader season. The hoped-for opportunities from several day trips in the waning days of deer season would not prove fruitful either. I started to question whether I was meant to shoot my first muzzleloader-deer with a flintlock, so on a one-day hunt with Duane "Bish" Bishoff, at the end of the 1989 season, I chose my T/C .54 caliber caplock rifle. I just wanted to see if it was destined to take a deer. Its twenty-eight inch barrel, being one inch across the flats, made it a stout, but not unwieldy.

Regardless of its heavy character, however, my shot was adversely affected by my chosen rest; namely, a hard window sill which caused the barrel to spring up.

I missed the deer, at fifteen yards, by a fraction of an inch. At that point my miss might just as well have been off by a foot. Then only a half an hour later, I made a shot on a grouse, with the same gun, only this time off hand (with no hard rest), and I took the bird in the neck at twelve yards. Oh! Now I was really kicking myself. How I could have missed that big deer, but hit that little grouse? Ahhhhh!

A number of years later when reading about Morgan's Riflemen, I realized why I missed my shot. Among the Riflemen, they knew about something they described as "barrel springing," [18] which is due to the barrel resting on a rigid surface with no give. The barrel actually jumps up a bit from the hard surface even with a moderate charge.

These Revolutionary War riflemen, therefore, liked to rest their rifles on soft moss, a hat or some other item that would soften the spring of the barrel during ignition.

Even though I could not seem to connect with a deer, that miss would be a well earned lesson, which taught me not to rest my gun or barrel on the edge of a board, plywood, rock or frozen ground, but rather to rest my rifle on my hand, or hat or something soft to dampen the vibration.

After the deer season, I went out a number of times for small game and, as had happened many times before, it seemed that on almost every foray I walked up on one or several deer. The deer would stand there looking at me or had no clue I was there. It was so ironic, and at the same time aggravating.

In the end I had to laugh at the irony; otherwise I would have driven myself mad by asking, *"Why could this not happen in one of the areas open for muzzleloading deer season?"*

The only thing to take my mind off of the missed quarry would be hunting small game from December until the end of February. I also looked forward to the next project, whether it was making clothing, camp accoutrements or some item for shooting. In preparing for the summer rendezvous schedule, there was always round ball to run as well as washing and cutting fabric into strips for patching. Repairing holes and adding a second sole to moccasins seemed like a never-ending task. Any time there was inclement weather and I was stuck inside, I usually mended stuff needed for camp.

With my maintenance done, I could concentrate on shooting and other competitions instead of having to miss an event on the shooting line because I was tending to repairs.

I also did this same maintenance for my time in the woods, making sure to have a good flint fitted in the jaws of the cock. I made sure my horn would continue to keep my powder dry and kept my bullet bag "topped off" at thirty-plus balls. In addition to that, I wanted one or two pairs of moccasins ready for a lot of walking. Just in case, however, I kept several needles and some thread in my belt pouch for necessary repairs to moccasins, clothing or gear even "on the trail."

My backpack or haversack generally held snacks of chocolate, raisins, and several apples as well as a tin boiler for making hot tea.

These purposeful preparations for woodsy forays gave me a sense of readiness for all of my hunts, but especially deer hunting. Making sure my gear was ready had the collateral effect of dispelling any anxiety to wonder *if* I was ready. Thus, I could concentrate on hunting, rather than lamenting the lack of some item or snack. Though there seems to be a number of small things to tend to, the overall picture was, and continues to be, a simple one, *"if you are prepared for the worst, you are never disappointed."*

Chapter 9
Focusing on the Fowler

During the spring of 1990 I headed to the farm to help my uncle with planting and general maintenance. While at the farm I used the fowler to shoot pigeons as they flew out of the barn and further taught my new pup, a retriever-springer mix named Gabe, to fetch birds. Both the fowler and Gabe performed well. Using Deerfoot, as in years past, I continued to do my best in keeping the farm yard clear of pests like woodchucks.

At this time I was invited to take a short trip to South Dakota with my grandmother and aunt to visit my grandfather's cousin. There I met the next door neighbors, the Christiansons who happened to have buffalo. After some friendly conversation and a little importuning I had an invitation to shoot the next one sometime that winter.

I continued to work until late May when Gabe and I headed back to the lake. I spent my time from then on studying for the bar exam, again, and shooting my new smooth bore along with Deerfoot, and accompanying pistol. After the exam I headed back to the lake and worked with my two main long guns.

When early September rolled around, I packed up my home made tent, rendezvous stuff, Gabe and Deerfoot and headed to the Eastern Primitive Rendezvous in Big Poole, Maryland. I was there for nine days, after which I drove another seventy-five miles further to the home of my youth in Fairfax, VA, where I stayed with my mother and step dad.

While there, I earned money from the neighbors by using my chain saw to cut down and cut up troublesome trees.

Focusing on the Fowler

After about a week, I headed north to Maine, with the two of them for six days and nights on my first windjammer cruise. Spending a week on the old Schooner, the J. & E. Riggin, moved me to consider the additional dimension of travel in the eighteenth century, especially when I assisted the captain & crew; the same as if I were a deck hand.

When the schooner made port at several islands with antique shops, the few muzzleloaders I found in them were New England fowling pieces, with deep heavy buttstocks. I do not believe I ever saw a single muzzleloading rifle in the shops.

In this country, during the 18th century, the smooth bore fowler reigned supreme. It gave me reassurance that I had assembled my smooth bore as a flintlock similar to the historic tradition of being carried by the common farmer, American Indian, hunter, or fisherman. If need be, my fowler could be used to hunt everything from grouse and squirrels to buffalo and elk. Though it was not on the trip with me, I would be using it as soon as I got back to Minnesota. I reflected on the fact that it was a versatile gun, made all the more desirable by the fact that I could use a rock to fire it.

Some have used the phrase that, *"There are no percussion caps lying on the ground, but there are pieces of flint or agate that can be knapped to satisfy that simple need."* I actually knapped a few rocks just for this gun and, though they might not have worked as well as a finely knapped English flint, I was *not* left with a gun that I could not fire.

The smoothbores of the eighteenth century were used in that territory to take squirrel, grouse, ducks, geese, turkey, deer, bear and moose. Essentially the type of game dictated whether the hunter loaded shot or round ball. Also, it has been documented that hunters often began a hunt loaded with "duck-shot" (i.e. No. 5 or 6 shot) and then upon seeing a moose would pull the top wad, collect the shot, and quickly load a round ball, followed by a wad on top.[18] Then the moose would be shot, or at least shot at with a large projectile capable of killing it.

At the end of the sailing trip, we headed back to Fairfax, Virginia, and several days following that, Gabe and I began the long road trip back to Minnesota.

We finally arrived home in mid September and within a week we were readying ourselves for a primitive black powder hunting and shooting camp, but not before a short hunting foray with my good friend Donnie Bergstrom.

The first thing he kicked up was a grouse and yelled to me to get ready, which I did. That shot seemed to go off in slow motion and when I was done swinging there was white smoke hanging in the air and a dead grouse on the ground, the first upland game I had taken with the fowler.

Donny exclaimed, *"You got him!"* as he picked up the bird and then added, *"I think you hit him with the whole load. Wow! and with a flintlock too!"*

It was a fun hunt that afternoon and made me excited for the upcoming camp a week and a half away. That camp was at a place called The Barn in LaPorte, MN, on property owned by Bob and Wanda Odegaard. It was surrounded by good grouse habitat.

I arrived early at The Barn on Thursday and after setting up my tipi, in preparation for the weekend, Gabe and I headed into the woods. In no time we had three birds using the flintlock fowler.

After we traipsed all over the woods that day, my neck and shoulder were sore from the thin braided strap on my shot pouch. As soon as I got back to the cabin I was determined to replace it with a much wider strap of heavy leather which would spread out the pressure from the weight of the pouch, especially when full of shot.

Aside from the discomfort of the shot pouch I enjoyed a lot of activities. During the weekend I shot most of the competitions with Deerfoot, but also made good use of the fowler and my flintlock pistol. With a full complement of firearms, what more did I need? Perhaps...more clothing.

As I considered my clothing used for hunting, I felt a cloth hunting frock (dyed red) was a necessity. This garment would wrap around my torso (right under/left over) and be secured with a sash and belt. I made sure to put "pulled fringe" on the shoulders, around the arms and all around the outside edges as was done two hundred years prior.

In using the new frock, I quickly found that the outside wrap of the hunting frock was a quick and handy pocket for items like a hand warmer or handkerchief. The use of the frock as an extra pocket, I later learned, was referred to as a "wallet," that is to say a small wall against the body. This set-up complemented my hunting/shooting exercises with a muzzleloader.

Almost Touching Success

I camped that year with fellow rendezvouser Swamper in his tipi for the opening weekend of Muzzleloader deer season. We were joined by Roger Cook (the owner of the first flintlock I ever shot) and another hunter by the name of Blue. We were in the woods all day, every day for four days and moved some deer, but I could not connect with one.

My one shot at a deer occurred as the deer was moving through a hazel thicket; and of course I had a deflection. Though I could not have done anything about the hazel thicket, I could have whistled or called out with a sharp "*hey*!" A sudden sound might have caused the deer to stop long enough to find a hole and take the shot. With only one round, the first shot is the most important.

Since that time I have learned to employ a "deer bleat" to slow down or stop a moving deer. Whether it is a "grunt-tube" or my voice, I have stopped many deer by bleating at them. Just such a bleat, on that day, might have given me an edge by making the deer pause for three or four seconds.

Anyone who has heard a sheep bleat and can mimic the sound with their own voice and use it in the deer woods (*owaah*, or *mmaaah*, or *nnaah* any of these sounds can be made with the human voice). Even if it is not one hundred percent sure to work, it can distract the deer and stop them long enough to put the gun sights on a non-moving animal. I was gaining experience a little at a time with the cost being, no deer to claim.

Following that weekend, I received an urgent call from John Christianson; the four year old bull had just killed a calf. If I wanted to shoot a buffalo, I had two days to get down to South Dakota. On Thursday morning, before sunrise, I headed down to Woonsocket, SD with Gabe and my 12 ga fowler. I was able to shoot the buffalo, which is a story in and of itself, and five days later was back at the cabin. Though Deerfoot also accompanied me on my first buffalo hunt in 1990, I did not use it. It was my constant companion along with Gabe. The reality is, I actually shot my first buffalo with my 12-gauge flintlock fowler, before I shot a deer with Deerfoot.

After butchering half a buffalo with my "cousin" Tim Arnquist and cleaning the hide and skull, I was ready to finish the balance of the deer season.

On the last weekend of the season, I recall one drive in particular. I had a fresh charge, a patched home-molded round ball seated over the powder. The frizzen was clean, and I was primed with FFFFg. I was ready when I saw the deer approach from the right, but it was an eighty-yard shot at a minimum. I took aim, touched the trigger and the rifle cracked off with no hesitation, but my shot occurred just as the deer began to move. The deer's rump shuffled a bit and then it ran. I quickly reloaded using the maple block and stood and waited for at least five minutes before one of the drivers came through.

It was a quarter to four and late in the day, when we gathered for a parlay. I thought my shot may have hit the deer in the hock. Try as I may, I could not convince anyone in the hunting party that it was my ball which had broken the deer's hock resulting in a blood trail. The six of us conferred for a few minutes more, at which point I offered to help run down the deer. The head of the party and his buddy, both looked at my flintlock (they both were using caplocks) and simply said,

"Naw. You might as well stay here. We got this."

So then I offered to flank on the high ground.

The reply was, "I wouldn't even bother, but you can if you want." They immediately headed off at a trot, following the blood trail.

So I ran flank in the off chance it, or another deer, might come my way, but after ten minutes a shot rang out. I cocked my rifle and waited for several minutes looking for any movement coming my way. Then I heard a *war-whoop*, a sure sign they had gotten the deer. I walked in the direction of the shot and met them and tagged the deer. We dragged it out to the logging road and gutted it there. The one who shot it took the heart, and no one objected when I asked to claim the liver. I took the deer home, butchered it, froze it and a week later we met to divvy up all three deer from our hunt. Though I was very grateful for the deer meat that we all had worked to acquire, I felt my contribution was minimal, because I should have dropped it.

In the grand scheme of things, I would rather be hunting deer than be in the office. I love to hunt deer from a stand, from a blind, still hunting and stalking. I enjoy helping others with deer drives, dragging their deer, helping to track deer, even run them down in a pinch. At the end of that particular season, however, I was not able to claim the honor of taking a deer with a muzzleloader. That afternoon I felt the immense weight of frustration from all the prior years wearing on me. Now this, and no one thought I had a hand in hitting the deer.

However, before I became too negative, I realized there lay an opportunity right in front of me to swallow my pride, and be thankful for the deer. My consolation rested in the thought that getting the wounded deer was much more important than who had shot it. Every time my "missed shot" began to nag at me, I resorted to telling myself, *"At least we got the wounded deer."* This is most certainly true.

If there is one thing I was beginning to understand about deer drives, is that the deer will most likely be on high alert and a bit anxious. Their propensities tended toward moving instead of stopping; running instead of walking. What I lacked, in comparison with others, was my own pool of experiences with deer. Though I was gaining experience, it seemed like a slow process.

I tried not to lament my deficiencies, but every time

Focusing on the Fowler

I compared myself with others, a depressed mood was inevitable. I knew I was a decent woodsman as I had walked up on deer too many times to prove otherwise, yet that never seemed to happen during the muzzleloader season!

Deer drives should be a team effort. Everyone participates in driving at some point, and everyone should also get an opportunity to be a stander, in position to shoot the deer as they come by or near the stander. I have nothing against deer drives per se, as they are usually productive.

Drives, however are not the only way to see deer. I also like to be sitting still when others move through the woods. Those who are "going in" for coffee, or lunch, as well as, heading back out to the stand, will unwittingly move deer. Deer bumped in this fashion are most apt to walk to a different area to feed or bed down.

In general, I had helped in many deer drives and usually, at the end of the season, received some deer meat for my efforts. I also received a deer hide or two for tanning.

As for the deer I had personally taken with modern firearm and archery, I had tanned the hides and fashioned them into clothing such as: jackets, pants, choppers, and moccasins as well as bags and pouches too numerous to count. I perceive deer as a source of both meat and hide.

I looked forward to preparing meat and tanning a hide from my own deer taken with a flintlock. I could then fashion the leather into some useful item for my historical outfit. I yearned for an opportunity to be alone in the woods on my terms, no drives or pushes, just me, no one else.

I was determined to take a deer by my own God-given skill and do it with my .45 caliber flintlock rifle. For now, however, I would have to wait and so would Deerfoot. At least I had some deer meat and about 45 pounds of buffalo;

so I was in pretty good shape.

Other Preparations and Adjustments

The utility and accuracy of Deerfoot was due, in no small part, to my ability to shoulder and line up the sights quickly and comfortably. On the English fowler, however, I found it necessary to add a back sight or ramp at the tang to raise the alignment of the front sight because it initially shot too low. There was also the added problem of shooting slightly to the left, (because of this I had to shoot the buffalo twice). I managed to use the fowler with this added ramp, but the set-up bothered me, as the ramp also had a notch decidedly to the right of center to account for the left-windage. I would rather be able to comfortably shoulder the piece, and by sighting straight down the plain of the barrel, have my bead or sight line up naturally with the tang.

This is especially true when shooting flying objects. After making a number of enquires to several gunsmiths, I really had no options other than bending the barrel to a point where it would shoot straight and level. I decided to give it a try.

I had read about "U" shaped bending-jigs, which spread the bend from the muzzle back as much as two thirds of the length of the barrel, towards the breech. In my case, the barrel being thirty-six inches, dictated that I make the jig about twenty-four inches long.

The wooden base or bottom of the jig consisted of a 2 X 6 board. At either end were perpendicular 2 x 6 uprights fourteen inches tall. Each of the uprights had a hole drilled about three inches from the top end of the wood, to accommodate the barrel being slipped in from one direction. The uprights were attached by means of box joints and the addition of steel corner braces. The inside spread of the uprights was about twenty-four inches. In the middle of the base was a spot for a bottle-jack, the type used for automobiles, with short pieces of wooden 1 x 6 as book ends to keep the jack centered. The base of the jig was then clamped to a table with "C" clamps at either end for stability and to prevent the base from bowing.

The barrel was inserted into the jig with several buffers to prevent kinking and spread the bend more evenly. The most effective buffers were a combination of a paint roller-through which the barrel was inserted, and a piece of wood 1/2" x 2" x 5" long between the jack saddle and the paint roller. I taped the wood to the roller and put tape on the barrel to mark either end of the roller. By centering the jack saddle in the middle of the roller, I was assured that the pressure would be at the same place (aka "centerline-radius point") on the barrel. I also put tape on the "intrados" (inner wall of the bend receiving the pressure) side of the barrel. In this case the barrel shot low and to the left so I had to apply pressure to the opposite side of the barrel, essentially high and to the right. This piece of tape on the intrados side was always placed down so that the barrel would distort in the same direction.

I used a common screw-type bottle-jack with an open "nut," protruding from a spigot at the base of the jack. The protruding nut was twisted to raise the jack-saddle until it firmly pressed against the wood/roller/barrel. From this point I counted the twists, or rather, half-twists due to their smaller increments. I was surprised to find just how far the barrel would distort before it held even the slightest bend.

I removed and refitted the barrel to the stock about eight times. As I increased the amount of distortion, the desired bend also increased. Once I had the desired windage/elevation to a point where the shots were hitting at the center of the target and below the bulls eye, I moved the centerline-radius to the top of the barrel, to raise only the elevation.

This process of distortions took four more sessions. I made sure to slightly over bend the barrel so it was shooting about two inches high, when sighting dead-on at 30 yards. Then I re-bent it back a bit to relieve the stress in the steel. This took two more sessions. When finished, it shot about a half-inch high at 30 yards, sighting dead-on.

The whole process took over five hours. It was not a job to be rushed and great precautions were taken to avoid a kinked barrel. I shot three round groups in each session to get a good average of the point of impact. I then swabbed the barrel clean to remove all fouling and provide the same conditions for the barrel in each of the sessions.

I figured that the stock would eventually yield its own downward tension to that of the barrel. A year later, sure enough, the gun was shooting, on average, one inch high at thirty yards. It has been stable ever since that time. It shoots consistently, sighting from center of the tang to the front sight, no ramps, no notches, no unwanted windage.

I have enjoyed a much greater degree of satisfaction shooting this flintlock smoothbore than I ever did with the caplock 20 gauge interchangeable barrel. My determination to use flintlocks for all my muzzleloading activities began with Deerfoot. It influenced me to expand my experience to include a historically styled smooth bore in the form of an English Fowler. I have never regretted that decision.

Focusing on the Fowler

Top-Author with Gabe, after successfully bagging three grouse - hanging from the belt - with the 12 gauge fowler; standing in front of his homemade tipi. Bottom-The heavy leather shot pouch with a newly fitted, two-inch wide strap. The wider strap displaces the four to five pounds of shot more comfortably.

My Journey with Deerfoot

Top-Author's first buffalo, the English Fowler in hand.
Bottom-A simple sketch of a bending jig, showing the intended placement of bottle twist-jack. The barrel is represented by the dotted line above the jack. The barrel only slips into the uprights from one side. A smaller hole for the muzzle on the left, a larger hole for the breech to the right.

Chapter 10
A Breath of Fresh Air

The following year, 1991, was a year of changes for many reasons. Firstly, in the spring, I hired a coach, the late Jerry Strauss, an incredible Jewish attorney who was brimming with energy. He made study of law fun. About two months after hiring Jerry, I went to stay with my relatives the Schulz's in Edina, MN until late July.

Each day I studied at the Edina public library; treating it like a job. When I took my breaks I perused the books and reference materials and found their resources in history were overwhelming. Every other day I checked out a different video or book on historical sites, and expeditions. My time in the Twin Cities parlayed into a study of the law *and* history.

Finally, on Thursday and Friday, July 25th & 26th, I sat for the exam. Several months crept by before I learned about my passing score. On the 25th of October, I was licensed and would be working soon thereafter.

A few days after the exam, I spent that Saturday with my godparents Julian and Jewel Arnquist, in South St. Paul. While there, it just so happened that a local TV station aired *The Gunsmith of Colonial Williamsburg*, a video featuring Wallace Gusler filmed back in 1967-8. It was the first time I had ever seen it and I was positively awestruck.

Wallace forged a rifle barrel, gun lock and other iron pieces from flat skelps of wrought iron. (Skelp is an old term for "beaten" or "slap," in this case, wrought iron beaten into a strip) He poured brass for the furniture then cleaned and polished each piece to a mirror finish. He cut out the stock from a maple plank, inlet the barrel, lock, trigger and the rest of the furniture into it. He then carved the wood and engraved the metal resulting in a beautiful .58 caliber flintlock rifle. The production compressed 200 man-hours into 59 minutes. (In 2000 while in Colonial Williamsburg, VA with my family I would get to hold that very rifle.)

On Sunday morning, I packed and headed back to the Cabin. At my first stop I retrieved Gabe, who had been cared for by my neighbor Rob Grooms, during my absence. (I am so thankful for the kindness of neighbors) Gabe was positively ecstatic and would not let me out of his sight for days.

Secondly, several days after my return, I got my buffalo hide back from the tannery. It was much anticipated and I used it for everything from moccasins to belts.

Thirdly, I read in the living history periodical, *Smoke and Fire*, that filming was being done for the movie **Last of the Mohicans**. Though I was ready to head out to North Carolina, I called one of the production managers who told me that the majority of production filming was done. All that remained was "mop-up" filming. Most of the extras had been there and gone, so I decided to stay home.

During that same time, I had a subscription to, **Muzzleloader Magazine,** in which appeared Mark A. Baker's column, *A Pilgrim's Journey*. In his column Mark shared his research on the clothing and accoutrements of the eighteenth century backwoodsman. Just as importantly, he tested his findings by "trekking" into the deep woods on foot, by canoe and on horse-back. As I read each issue, I was inspired by his dedication to historical accuracy. Seven months or so later, Mark wrote about training Daniel Day Lewis for his flintlock shooting and loading on the run.

The more I read, the more my perceptions changed. My epiphany, about historical correctness, however, did not come all at once, but slowly over time after I began to scrutinize my own clothing and accoutrements. I had assumed (wrongly, perhaps arrogantly) that my clothing was good enough to be "correct" for the period that I was portraying. I had camped out in the woods in all four seasons, with my homemade gear. It had worked more or less, but the more I studied, the more I could see that my clothing and some accoutrements would not have existed in the period.

I did not change everything all at once, but rather with each new piece of insight, I only focused on a small portion of my gear at a time. Deerfoot, for instance, occurred, because I was trying to emulate an earlier time period. Later, my conversion from caplock to flintlock occurred because I was ready to try an older historical ignition. Each revelation was a small step. Earlier in March, I had acquired (from Keith Johnson of Bemidji, MN), an eighteenth century styled tomahawk with a hammer poll. Though the style would not have caught my attention a year earlier, now it jumped out at me as a more proper accoutrement for my portrayal. (My transformative efforts took the better part of the decade, but by 1997-98 I had substantially altered my interpretation.)

That fall, 1991, for the third year in a row, I headed out to work at the family farm for several weeks in September followed by three weeks at the sugar beet dump in October. When working 12 to 14 hour days, there was no time to spend my money, but before I departed North Dakota, I purchased a lamb from my foreman, Lyle Ladwig, and brought it home in the back of my truck...alive.

When I arrived back home, I put it in the only pen I had, until it rammed its head into the door and almost broke the bracing. Then I figured I might just as well slaughter it that evening instead of waiting until next morning and risk losing it.

I loaded up Deerfoot and dispatched with one shot to the heart lung area, followed by gutting, quartering and hanging it. I also set aside a few pieces from the back-strap for the maple-wood fire I had kindled in the grill.

By 8:30 that evening I was enjoying grilled lamb chops and I ate until I was stuffed like a "fat-tick." That lamb carried me through to January, but, just around the corner, I would be adding more meat to the larder.

The Fruits of a Good Hunt

Later that same fall, my friends Duane "Bish" Bischoff and "Uncle Zeb", invited me on a muzzleloader hunt (beginning the last weekend of November) in Paul Bunyan State Forest, between the towns of Bemidji and Akeley, Minnesota.

The arrival of the muzzleloader opener was accompanied by blustery winds, with temperatures hovering at five degrees above zero. The three of us headed out into separate areas of the woods to walk into the wind and see if a deer could be caught off guard. After an hour or so of scouting, I could see that some deer were moving, but did not put eyes on any, so I headed back to camp.

I continued, from the prior year, my use of short wool leggings that tied below my knee and over my pac-boots. The addition of these to my legs prevented snow from collecting in the top of my boots where it would melt and remain uncomfortably wet and cold.

In the past I had made use of buckskin pants and wool pants, of my own manufacture, the cuffs of which barely fit over my boots. The problem, however, was the "ledge" created by the top of the boot, where the pant-leg bulged out collected snow which melted. The short leggings worn on my early morning jaunt kept my calves and shins warm and dry, but there was a draw-back. In deeper snow, not only did my knees and thighs remain unprotected from snow and precipitation, but the snow now collected on the cuff of the legging just below my knee. The circumstance moved me to consider alternatives; and the answer, in the form of full length leggings, was not far off.

    I arrived back at camp and figured that the others had already been there and gone. I took some time for a quick bite, and then headed out into the wintery woods and a stiff wind. I was not enthused about the conditions, but not altogether discouraged either. I reminded myself that we had three full days ahead of us. The area had a good population of deer which had not felt the pressure of the regular season several weeks earlier.

    Moreover, I had my rifle in good working order, plenty of powder, round balls and good flints. The more I considered these things, the more eager I became. I kept that thought foremost in my mind, as I slowly crept to my stand. A positive attitude made my time spent in the blustery chill of blowing snow much more acceptable. I was indeed alone. My closest companion, was at least a quarter mile away, sitting on his stand.

    I had maintained my vigil on the stand for about an hour when I saw the hind end of a deer as it walked away from me and even though I was not able to shoot it, I became excited. That brief sight of a deer walking unmolested, rather than bounding away from drivers, was encouraging. It was all I needed to endure more time in the stand and fight off the cold, waiting for another to appear.

    After thirty minutes or so I saw in my periphery a

leaf that kept bouncing, or rather rotating. When I turned to look for the moving object, I had a difficult time locating it. I continued to scan the woods and when I caught sight of the "leaf" again I realized it was an ear that quickly materialized into a deer. Seconds later, it emerged from a low spot pausing occasionally to feed. It appeared close enough for a shot, and remained broad-side. So far, so good.

Suddenly, I forgot about the cold and wind. I gently maneuvered into position to shoot, removed the lock cover and rested the rifle on my knee. The slim .45 was balanced nicely just forward of the trigger guard. I waited a short time for the deer to take several steps out of a clump of hazel whips and then took aim, set the back trigger and several seconds later I touched the front trigger. The flintlock rifle cracked off with no hesitation, and, through the smoke, I saw the deer go down!

I clambered to stand up as quickly as possible, while holding onto Deerfoot in my left hand. Instinctively I grabbed my powder horn and un-stoppered it. I filled the powder measure, dumped it into the barrel and then, using my maple loading block, pushed a patched round ball into the barrel. I drew the ramrod and pushed the ball all the way home.

I glanced up to see that the deer was still down before I primed the pan and shut the frizzen. I was ready again. When I saw the deer try to rise up, I shot again. I reloaded, but I climbed down from the stand before I primed.

Once on the ground, I lost sight of the deer so I side-stepped slowly to determine the direction it had moved. I realized that it had turned around trying to go back down into the low spot, but was using its front legs only. I trotted through the shin-deep snow to a small rise which afforded a full view of the deer. I was excited and trying to remain calm, so I used a tree for a brace. I shot a third time, but could tell my shot deflected. I reloaded, and walked up to the place where the deer had been earlier. I could see a clipped stub of hazel from my second shot on the stand.

Shooting in hazel thickets can be a roll of the dice. The thin whips blend into the color of the deer hair so well that one does not realize they are in the way until after the shot. The tough, stringy nature of hazel makes it a formidable hindrance, second only to ironwood (hop hornbeam) whips.

By this time, I could see the deer was not going anywhere. It just laid there attempting to get up every couple of seconds. I reloaded and took my time in finding an opening through the brush and braced up to make a killing shot. Deerfoot cracked off its fourth shot and with that I had finally taken my first muzzleloader deer and what is more, I had taken it with a flintlock muzzleloader.

OH Joy! I stood there for several seconds ready to pinch myself. All I could seem to do was emphatically mutter the words, *"Yes, thank you, Lord,"* over and over again.

After basking in my euphoria for a short time, I knew I had better reload. I quickly put a strip of patching, to my mouth and shook a ball out of the ball bag. I placed the wet end of the patching on the muzzle, centered the ball and seated it with the pommel of my hunting knife. Following that, I cut away the patching, short started the ball, then rammed it all the way home with the ramrod. After priming the pan I tended to the maple loading block around my neck. It was empty from the last shot, so I cut and moistened three patches and inserted three new round balls into the block. As I sheathed my knife, I heard Bish call from a nearby ridge,

"Hey John, 'Whadjya' get?"

My Journey with Deerfoot

"A nice little button buck," I replied with satisfaction.

"Hey hey, alright!" Bish replied with a ring of congratulatory joy. *"Finally, you got your first muzzleloader deer. Way to go buddy! I'll give you a hand dragging it."*

The moment I had been waiting for was upon me. Finally, I had taken a deer with a flintlock. I was on my own. It was not the product of a drive. It had been feeding on its own, according to the natural rhythms of the woods. As I took my rosewood-handled, Odegard knife in hand and began to dress my deer, it felt like a victory lap. Upon removing the entrails, I separated out the heart and liver, cleaned them in the snow and bagged them, before I stowed them in my pack.

We dragged the deer out to the logging road and then to the camp. In my elated state, however, the mile long drag seemed like a short jaunt. In no time we had arrived at camp.

I had taken my first deer with a flintlock muzzleloader, and not just any rifle, but the very rifle that I had marked with the track of a deer. I felt that the slim .45 caliber rifle had finally earned its name Deerfoot and gave me the distinction of taking my first muzzleloader deer with a flintlock. Better yet, I had done so among supportive friends.

In the years following, my efforts included, Mark Sage and Gene Shadley, two of my closest friends and biggest supporters in shooting flintlocks. We had enjoyed a number of hunts and we would continue to do so; a welcomed difference from the unfortunate negativity of some folks, half a decade earlier. The personal decision each of us made to change from caplock shooting to a common interest in flintlocks, opened an exciting new door to many more historically based events, camps and hunts.

A Breath of Fresh Air

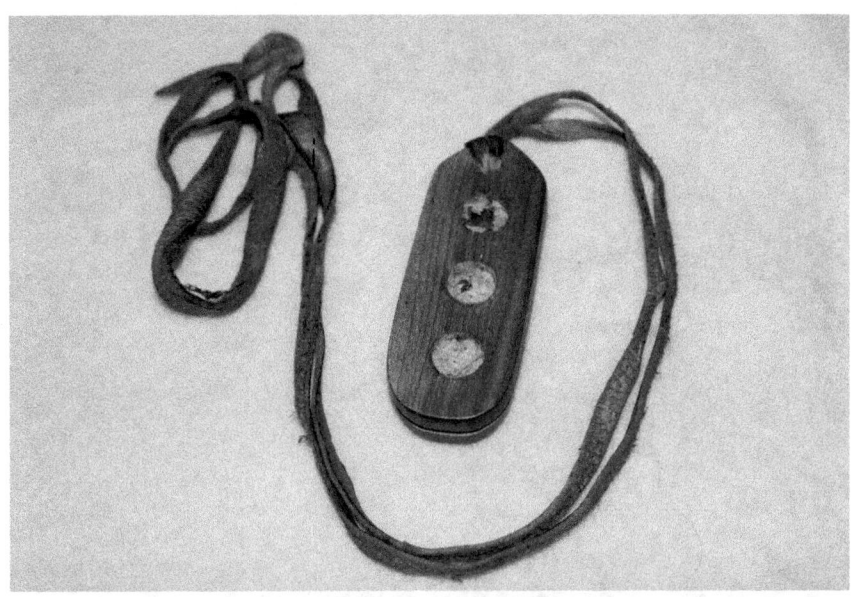

Top-Maple loading block filled with three round balls in greased patches ready to load into the barrel. The block hangs from the neck, within easy reach.

Bottom-Author's first flintlock deer, shot at 63 paces, with a home molded .440 round ball and 65 grs of FFFg, while hunting in the Paul Bunyan Refuge near Bemidji, MN.

My Journey with Deerfoot

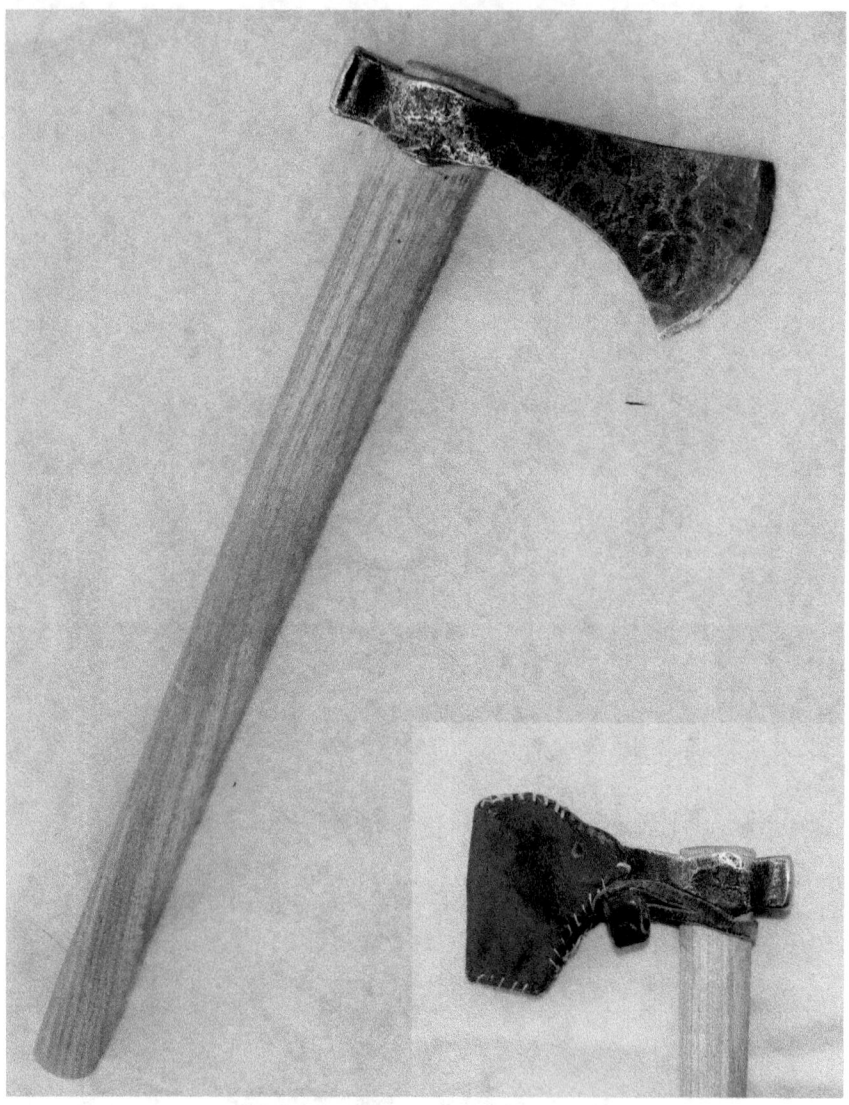

Poll Tomahawk carried by author from 1991 to present. It was fashioned by Keith Johnson, Bemidji, MN. It sports a punched eye with hardened steel bit and squared hammer poll. The cutting edge is 3-3/8" and overall length is 6-1/2." Overall width (at the eye) 1-5/8" and 1-1/16 thick at pole and ahead of the eye. Weight 1lb 3oz. The hickory handle 18" long.

Inset-When carried into the field, the tomahawk is covered with a scabbard to prevent being cut by the edge.

Chapter 11
The Next Horizon

With the advent of April of 1992, I decided to make some changes. The more I looked at my own portrayal of a colonial hunter, the more I considered a new form of tenting that would fit into the mid eighteenth century or shortly thereafter. My first decision, was to determine if I could sell the tipi. I put the word out among my friends and in no time I had a buyer for the whole thing. I used the sales proceeds to purchase a 9' x 11' wedge tent with a 4' bell-back. This type of shelter aligned more closely with the type of shelter used during colonial times, but my efforts did not stop there.

I took on several new projects, one of which was a late eighteenth century caped hunting frock. This new one was made of light canvas, dyed green and it sported pulled fringe all around; a style that would be worn by a longhunter of the period. I spent the better part of the week preparing the cloth (washing/dyeing), cutting out the pattern, sewing and lastly pulling all the fringe on the cape, around the arms and around the opening.

Before I had time to breathe, it seemed, I also made two pairs of cloth pants, to be used at my new part time job, interpreting at The White Oak Fur Post, (a 1798 fur post north of Deer River Minnesota).

After completing both pairs, I dyed one brown and left the other white. These were a plain sort of garment an *"engagé"* or common employee of the Northwest Company would wear in the canoe.

Within a year, however, I altered the white pants into fall-front knee britches, which could be worn with or without leggings.

As if these several projects were not enough, I also wanted a wool waistcoat in the style of the 1770's. Since my hands were full with my law office part time and my interpreting job part time, I availed myself of the fine sewing services of Cindi Sage, Mark Sage's wife. I bought fabrics for the shell and liner, as well as eighteen buttons, and left it with her. Two weeks later I had a fitted, sleeveless waistcoat in a mottled green color, which I wore at the all the camps for many years thereafter. It has remained one of my favorites.

By the time the Kindred Rendezvous rolled around in mid-May, I had nearly all the fringe pulled on my new hunting frock. After I set up camp on Friday, I spent the better part of the evening pulling the remaining fringe (all the loose threads balled-up became excellent fire starter too).

That night as I reflected on my efforts to portray an eighteenth century man, I felt sense of progress; that my clothing, accoutrements, and shelter complemented my use of a flintlock firearm.

The next morning, my new tent decided to pull its own stakes in the rain and drizzle. My neighbor Darrel Kersting, who saw the tent topple, quickly came over and helped me set back up and re-stake.

It seems the tent, made of 10 oz. "boatshrunk-Sunforger," shrunk when it became wet (which helps repel water) and with that, the short stakes were pulled loose. Not to worry though, it was a quick lesson in the idiosyncracies of my new shelter and the need for longer stakes. Before the next camp, I made it a priority to cut new stakes from the "Y" branches of a maple I had dropped for firewood. These new stakes were two inches thick and over a fourteen inches long. One side of the "Y" was cut short as a catch-hook for the tent loops. The new stakes held up well before being replaced with tent pins of a historical design. The tent sheds water extremely well and it has been a good shelter for more than thirty years.

The more things change,
The more they stay the same

Not only was I changing the fashion of my clothing, but also my firearms. After shooting Deerfoot as my main rifle for nearly seven years, I began to consider as my third major project, a new rifle with a larger bore. The choice was based on my familiarity with Deerfoot which became my default reference, simply because I did not have any other flintlock longrifle to use for comparison.

By early summer 1992 I began to build a .54 caliber heavy iron-mounted Southern rifle, which would eventually become my "go-to" gun. It sported: a Forty-two inch straight octagon Green Mountain barrel, 15/16 across the flats, slightly figured maple stock, Davis double-set triggers, and plain iron ramrod pipes.

It was in many respects similar to Deerfoot, especially the total use of iron mountings. The differences in this new rifle were the Large-Siler Lock instead of the small one, and a much heavier caliber, better suited for bear and elk.

While assembling the rifle I raised it to my shoulder many times and concluded a butt plate with less curve would fit more comfortably. When it came time to install the butt plate, I halted assembly until I had an opportunity to use the charcoal forge at the White Oak site.

One day after work, I gathered some wood shavings, and fresh charcoal and with butt plate in hand, headed to the forge. After a few strikes with flint & steel, I placed the glowing char cloth into the wood shavings and fresh

My Journey with Deerfoot

charcoal. The bellows, typical of the time, were double chambered and produced a fairly constant stream of air flow. A dozen pulls on the long wooden stave that formed the bellows handle and the charcoal was glowing brightly.

I nested the butt plate in the center of the glowing charcoal and after working the bellows for a short while, the butt plate was a dull orange. I gently tapped it on the anvil with a mallet to straighten the curved shape and take out nearly all of the "crescent" shape. Before I let it cool, I made use of a small carpenter's square to verify that it was still true and not twisted.

I spent the next day carefully inletting and attaching the butt plate. The flatter shape did not require the removal of so much wood and by mid-day it was installed. I was glad that I had reworked the butt plate as I found the adjustment noticeably more comfortable to shoulder and shoot. The front and back sights were set up in a fashion similar to Deerfoot. Lastly, I treated the stock with aqua fortis [18] and linseed oil as I had seen Wallace Gusler do in the video.

After assembling the new rifle with a good deal more patience than I had done with Deerfoot, I converted my original shooting pouch from .45 caliber back to .54 caliber and began experimenting with different volumes of powder for big-game and small-game charges. Once I had determined the amount of my standard charge (67 grains FFg), I simply cut down to 45 grains for small game. For bear and elk, I added about fifteen percent more powder (75-80 grains FFg).

I intended to carry it deer hunting as my first shot and, on occasion, Deerfoot would accompany me as my back-up. My practice of carrying two rifles in the woods had an added benefit which moved me to make incremental changes in my equipage.

In an effort to protect Deerfoot from dirt and snow, I generally kept it in a gun-case made from a wool blanket. While it was cased, I could gently lay it on the ground, in the wet grass or snow if need be, without worrying about getting the lock area wet, muddy or dirty. I could still rotate it up to use it as a "Moses stick" allowing me to brace the .54 (which I later named Ultimus). On the several occasions when I needed a quick second shot, I slipped it out of the wool case with ease. This continues to be my standard procedure when carrying two rifles.

When carrying Deerfoot or my .45 pistol as a back-up, I kept an empty snuff container for the .45 balls and patches. However, the snuff can rattled incessantly, so I ended up using a small deerskin poke filled with .440 balls, accompanied by the .45 loading block, neither of which made any noise.

About that same time, I had purchased a 5/16 brass range rod and fitted it with a barrel saver. The smaller diameter rod and saver fit a little deeper into the .45 caliber muzzle and gave better protection to the muzzle and barrel. When necessary, I changed out jags to use a .45 jag for cleaning. For the most part, however, I kept that brass range rod fitted with the larger .530 jag to service the larger rifle.

With all the new changes to my clothing and equipage that summer, I was also looking forward to the new movie, **Last of the Mohicans**, due in theaters by September.

It just so happened, while interpreting early American history at the Hjemkomst Center in Moorhead, Minnesota, I accompanied some members from the Plainsmen Black Powder club, of Fargo ND, to see the movie.

Later that night and on into the next day, we

discussed that Hollywood had made use of folks who actually knew how to shoot flintlocks. It was inspiring that people viewing the movie could see just how fast a flintlock ignition is supposed to fire. It also showed how the rifle was the constant companion on foot, by horse or in a canoe.

We all knew what it took to run with a long gun in hand on flat ground, but to do so in the mountains was even more impressive. Little did I know that I too would be pursuing a buck on foot in the coming muzzleloader season.

Several months later I was in my stand, taking aim at a six point buck. My shot hit a low hanging ironwood branch and deflected. Though I had mortally wounded the deer, I felt the need to follow sooner than I would have liked, because there were other hunters in the area who might claim it if I did not get there first.

The whole affair took about forty minutes and in that time I ran up and down hills, through brush and finally down into a deep ravine, tracking my buck in eight inches of snow. In the end, I ran him down and dispatched him. That was my second deer taken with a flintlock.

I cannot deny that throughout the matter, thoughts of Hawkeye ran through my head. In the movies it looks easy, but in reality it can be terribly tiring. Even though I was tired, I kept repeating to myself, *"I'll rest when I get there,"* In the end, I needed a rest before I dragged it all the way back to camp...up hill, in the snow and ice.

Sharing the Experience with Pleasant Company

As 1993 dawned, more changes were on the horizon. The first item of business was to refit myself with a new belt knife. I had been looking for more of a "trade knife" shape with a drop heel, and happened upon a Dexter/Russell french cook's knife at the White Oak Rendezvous back in the Summer of 1992. As soon at I saw it on the blanket I purchased it with the thought of reshaping it.

I spent several hours at the grinder as I shortened the blade and narrowed the width being careful not to burn the blade. That was followed by removing the factory scales using a hacksaw to cut through the wood, but not cut into the tang. The cutler's rivets were also removed using a hacksaw to cut parallel to the tang. The new scales for the handle came from a piece of maple firewood at the lake cabin.

Next, I brought the collection of pieces to Gene Shadley, and showed him what I had in mind. In short order he attached a soft iron "bird-head" pommel and tightly fitted the maple scales in between the integral bolster and pommel; a week later I had it back in hand. I fashioned a sheath for it; and finished off the edges with some thong from one of my deer hides and I was in business.

Due to the sheath being differently styled than my former knife, the pommel now protruded noticeably and facilitated an easier removal from the sheath. This seemingly insignificant difference made my loading more streamlined. When I cut patches at the muzzle, I could quickly use the pommel to seat the ball. I used the new knife until I replaced it in 1999 with a Jack Hubbard knife, more closely akin to a provincial-made trade knife of the eighteenth century and a slightly different sheath with its own advantages.

The next item of business would be to address a small, but irritating, problem with Deerfoot. The threaded portion of the barrel breech was slightly longer than the breech plug which left a thread exposed on the inside of the barrel. The resulting gap at the breech would catch the cleaning patches and thus the ramrod would, on occasion, become stuck. The stuck ramrod really became a problem when I was out in the woods or at an event.

Since I did not carry my range rod with me into the woods, or on some of the rendezvous competitions, I resorted to my ramrod in the gun. When necessary I screwed a cleaning jag onto it. The problem ensued when I pushed the jag-end all the way down to the breech of the barrel and the cloth would become stuck on the exposed thread. My next operation generally required a set of snub-nosed pliers to grab the protruding end of the ramrod to extract it. The upside of that, however, is that now I generally carry a diminutive pair of pliers in my shooting bag and a standard pair, as a second, in my hunting pack. They have come in handy in a number of situations.

In the early summer of 1993, I finally brought the barrel to Jay Pagel, a crackerjack gunsmith in Grand Rapids, and requested his skill to solve the nagging problem. He lopped an inch off the breech end of the barrel to get rid of the pitted threads and he cut new threads. With that, he re-inserted the breech plug so the shoulder of the plug met firmly with the ends of the threads and the inside base of the bore. The result was, no gap. In less than two months I had the barrel back in hand.

I reinstalled the barrel, drilled new holes for the pins to attach the barrel, as well as re-fitted the muzzle cap to fit evenly with the shorter, forty-one-inch barrel. I drilled a new touch hole at or above the top of the pan. Following an afternoon of shooting, I happily cleaned the barrel with no stuck patches or jags.

As time went on, Deerfoot usually stood in the corner and out of the way. In late August, however, I brought it along to allow my girlfriend and future wife,

The Next Horizon

Connie Cutsforth, to try her hand at shooting a flintlock. I methodically showed her how to load and shoot Deerfoot numerous times until she wanted to go through the procedure on her own, that is to say, without my assistance... or my head peering over her shoulder.

Connie loaded the rifle, then propped it up on a set of crossed sticks in order to shoot paper targets and clays at various distances. We soon made a habit of driving out to a nearby gravel pit and spending all afternoon shooting. Deerfoot was not neglected, but functioned well as my soon-to-be-wife learned how to shoot a flintlock muzzleloader instead of a caplock. Even though Deerfoot was still used on squirrel hunts and the like, I began to hunt almost exclusively with the larger .54 caliber rifle.

After Connie and I were married in 1995, she continued to shoot it until early winter when she mentioned that I would be a father.

During her pregnancy and later while nursing, she did not want to handle the lead round balls. I was not sure when she would get back to shooting, but I kept it ready for her.

During Connie's "time-off," Deerfoot remained my second rifle during vigils in the deer stand. It was kept covered in the blanket case and hung on a hook within easy reach of my seat.

When I knew I would be spending time in the stand, I headed out with Ultimus in my right hand and Deerfoot in my left. It was my companion on a few more hunts as my back-up, the last of which was a deer hunt in a newly opened State Park hunt. As in the past, it hung out of the way unless and until it was needed. During that hunt it did in fact see some use.

On day three of the hunt, I had shot my second

deer with Ultimus, re-loaded and just after I had lowered Ultimus to the ground, two dogs approached on a deer trail. I remained in the stand, where I still had Deerfoot primed and ready. I knew if need be I could quickly pull up the .54 for an additional shot.

Rather than get down and have to defend myself and my downed quarry, I shouldered Deerfoot and waited for the dogs to approach closer. When they were about fifteen yards away, I opted to shoot a popple sapling leaning a foot or so above one dog's back. Aside from the one's occasional snarl at the other, all was still and quiet until I shot. With the combination of the gun's report, the smoke, the shattering of the wood, and the sapling bouncing off one dog's back, both dogs bolted from the scene like rockets. Problem solved!

Though my attention to Deerfoot had been occasional, it would eventually wean down to nothing. In the following year, 1998, I acquired another flintlock rifle, referred to as my "Virginia" rifle, also a .54. caliber. Having two rifles, of the same caliber afforded greater convenience. Thereafter, instead of bringing both .440 and .530 round balls, I carried only the .530 for both .54 caliber rifles. With my new Virginia rifle as my go-to, Ultimus became my back-up rifle, not Deerfoot.

Finally, I stored the trim .45, after oiling the barrel profusely, and wrapping it in oily rags, followed by plastic and lots of tape. I did not want it to rust if I was not going to use it. Frankly, I did not know when it would get used again. So, it sat in the corner, wrapped up for some unforeseeable time in the future, when I might pull it out of its cover.

Connie had not shot for some time and she rarely if ever asked about shooting any gun. As a consequence, it remained stored away. She had not lost her passion to shoot,

The Next Horizon

as we had planned to build a shorter rifle for her, but she had other obligations to manage like three children and a full-time job. On occasion, she shot my .22 caliber rifle and was a crack shot with it, but in reality, neither she nor I would pay any attention to Deerfoot for a number of years to come.

I would go on to shoot everything with my Virginia rifle from squirrels to deer, bear and elk, at which point Deerfoot was but a dim memory.

Prior to that, Deerfoot had performed admirably by: accurately spitting out more than three thousand shots, had endured one hundred degree heat and thick humidity, bitter sub-zero cold, endless rainy days, blowing snow, river muck, rust and swollen wood.

But now it sat all alone, wrapped up, not even visible to the eye. What had once been my constant companion, now sat waiting for a time when new energetic hands might bring it to bear once again on targets; or perhaps proudly display it in-hand at the rendezvous camps. One day it might take game again, in the tall woods. For the time being, however, Deerfoot would have to wait.

My Journey with Deerfoot

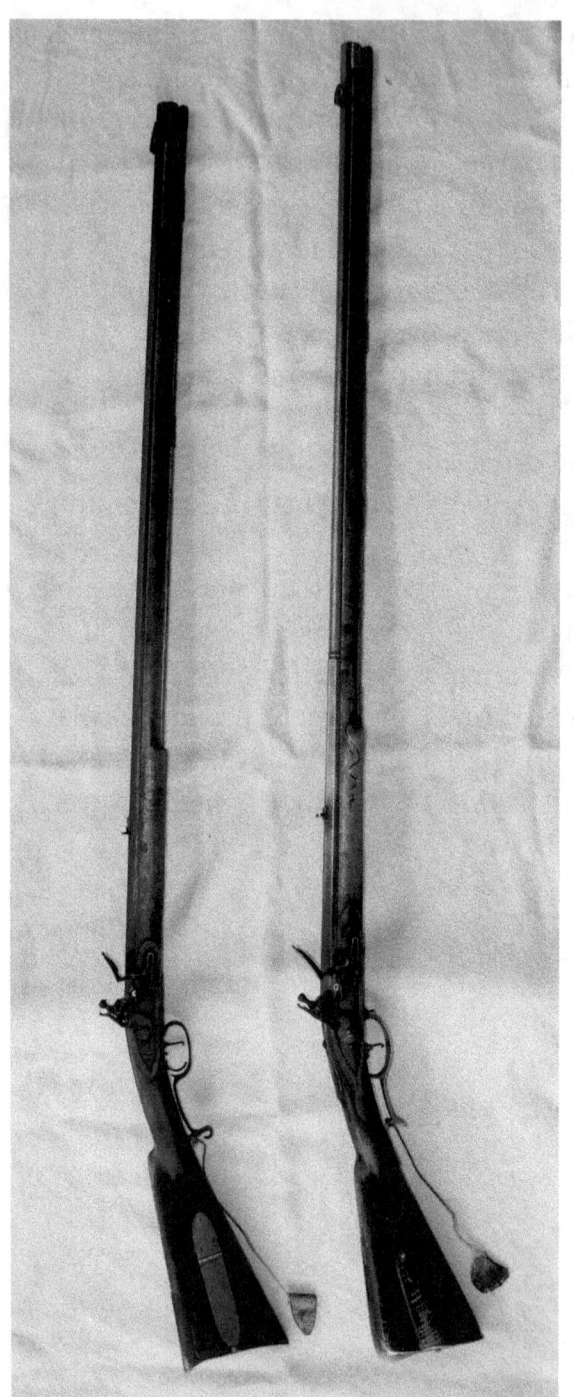

Top-Ultimus, the .54 caliber, heavy iron mounted southern rifle. It shares many characteristics with Deerfoot, but is heavier. Author used it to take a dozen more muzzloader whitetails and later his first elk.

Bottom-The Virginia rifle crafted by the late Glen Jones of Tremonton Utah. Glen worked, for a time, at Colonial Williamsburg as a gunsmith. The rifle was originally made in .54 caliber. Later, after thousands of rounds, it was bored out to .58 caliber and remains the author's main rifle for all types of hunting. Author has used it to take over four dozen whitetails, a number of bear, his second elk as well as his first and second mule deer.

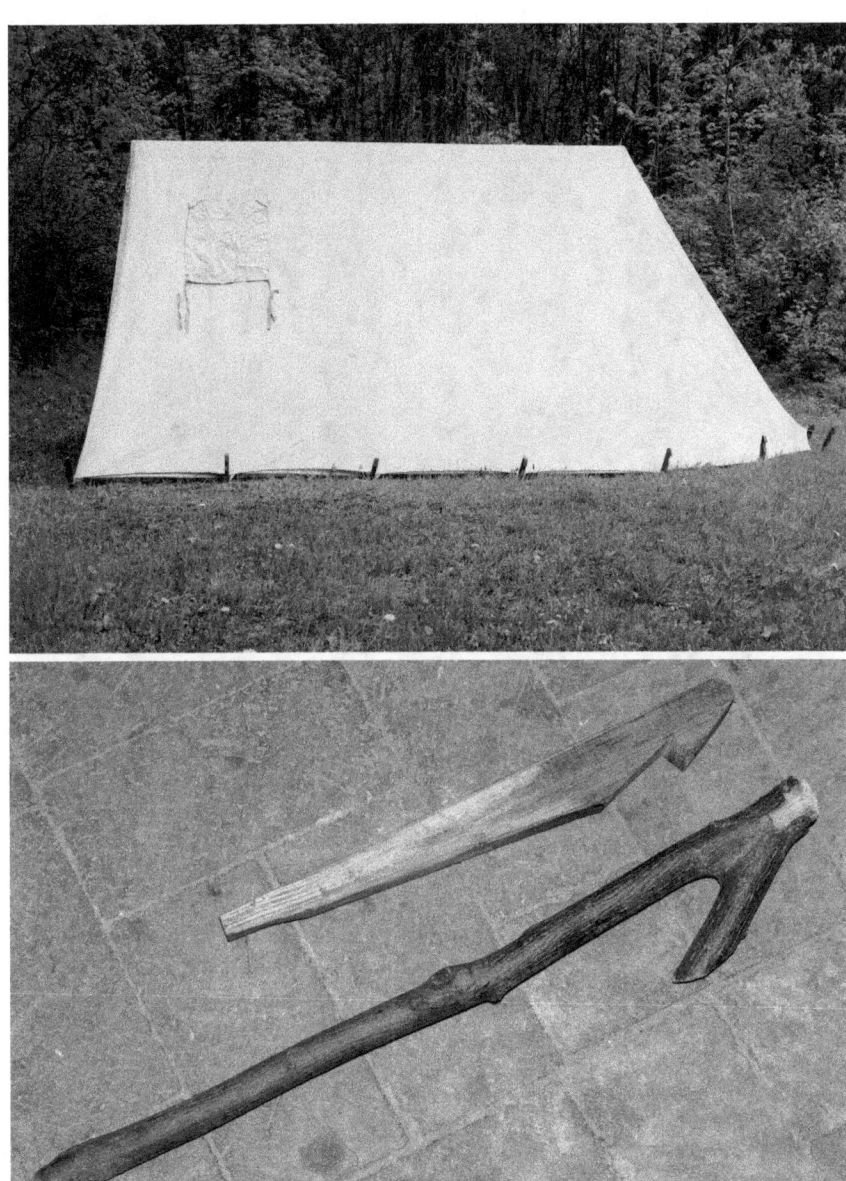

Top-18th century style 9' x 11' wedge tent, with a 4' bell back. Bottom-A period correct tent pin (upper) cut from a maple board. Author made pins of this type to replace the crude wooden stakes, like the example seen (lower), made from the "Y" of a hickory branch. For comparison the bricks are 3 3/4" x 8."

My Journey with Deerfoot

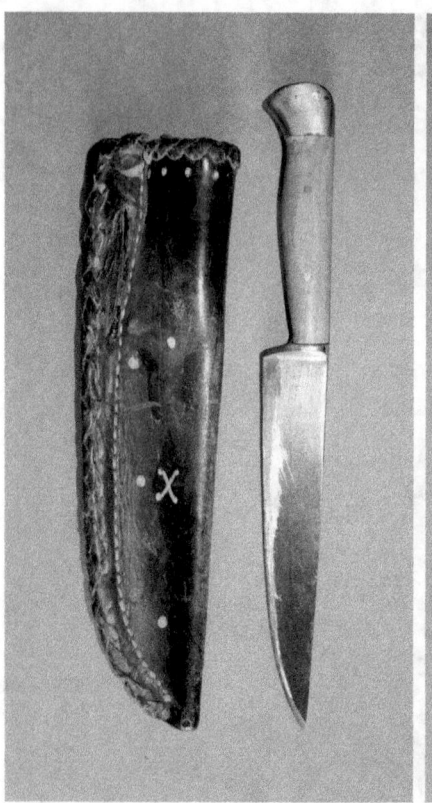
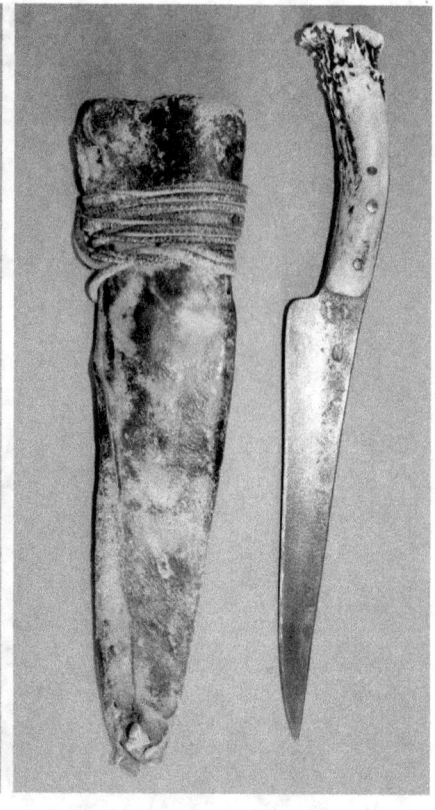

The progression of personal knives:
Left - The knife carried by author from 1993 to 1998 - Originally manufactured as a Dexter/Russel, Chef's knife with integral bolster. Author reworked the blade: cut it down to 7-1/4" from plunge grind to tip; 1-5/16" at the hilt. The handle, executed by Eugene Shadley, has a "bird's-head" pommel of soft iron; maple scales are secured by soft iron pins. The sheath is heavy vegetable tanned cow hide and finished at the edges with braided deer skin. The markings are Ojibwe. It is secured on the belt through the loop, left of the welted seam.

Right - An earlier 18th century style knife carried by author from 1998 to present - Crafted by Jack Hubbard of Kentucky. The blade is 7-3/4' long from ricasso/handle to tip; width at the drop-heal is 1-3/8" spine to edge. Handle is deer antler, secured by two copper pins peened over. The sheath is formed using rawhide cow for the inner body, then covered with soap-tanned elk. It is secured by inserting between the belt/sash and the body and tied. The tie is 4' and doubled over to provide one long and one short tie.

Chapter 12
Looking Backward, Looking Forward

As fathers, we dream of handing down to our children certain traditions which are near and dear to us. We hope to pass down our outdoor skills and knowledge like taking small game, upland birds, waterfowl and large game; fishing from a canoe and through the ice. It also includes methods of cleaning, butchering and cooking the game we harvest. It also encompasses simple tasks like gathering roots, berries and a host of other wild foods, but it does not stop there. We hope to hand down the very dirt we stand upon which may be the family farm, hunting property or lake cabin, as well as the personal property in the form of tools, knives, and guns.

While I watched my children grow, I envisioned them hunting with me and indeed they did follow me into the woods on numerous outings for squirrel and other game.

In order to give them the impression of carrying a gun in the woods, they carried mock-up rifles which I had made for them. These "rifles" helped cement safe handling of a firearm. During those years, any one of the three children would sit with me in the deer stand, deer blind or duck blind.

After the necessary attendance at hunter safety and gun safety classes, they would be old enough to handle guns that shot bullets and round balls. Again, that would take time.

Sarah the eldest took her classes for gun safety and shot several of my rifles with a good deal of enjoyment. I could tell, though, it was not her top priority. She enjoyed shooting BB guns and the occasional .22, but rarely mentioned muzzleloaders. There were several occasions in which she heard me shoot at squirrels, prompting her to poke her head out to see where I was. On one occasion she called out.

"Hey dad! Do you want me to let Gabe out?"

"Yeah, that would be good." I responded. "He can track a squirrel if it's wounded."

She let out Gabe, who promptly tracked the squirrel. Right on his heels was, Sarah, not necessarily ready to shoot, but wanting very much to be a part of the action. Johannah was not far behind trying to fit her foot into her boot. John was in the rear, his coat half-on and his exposed arm chasing the open sleeve behind his back. All three followed Gabe, who had the squirrel pinned underneath a stump. It was a good hunt.

In the early years, both Jo and John exhibited a gentle competition between themselves; both shot accurately too. I mentored each of them in loading *and* reloading muzzleloaders under controlled conditions and familiarized them with the basics at an established firing line.

Johannah's desire to shoot flintlocks was more subdued than her brother John's. There were times when she would ask to follow along during a hunt only because she wanted to see what her big sister, Sarah, was doing; and at other times "Jo" wanted to spend time with Dad. She often watched quietly as I loaded and shot the flintlock; not saying much, she simply observed. When it was her turn to load and shoot on the range, she shot quite accurately, but she did let me know she was not overly fond of the black powder fouling that found its way onto her hands during reloading.

I must say, however, I have never known her to be squeamish. Rather, she was and has always been eager to lend a hand with gutting and dragging deer on numerous occasions. I am so proud of her for that.

Looking Backward, Looking Forward

As for John, like most boys, he was eager to do "dad stuff." Then again, he enjoyed shooting all sorts of guns from the eighteenth to twenty-first century. He eagerly observed me as I loaded the flintlock and I could tell, based upon his questions, he was taking mental notes. He was always eager for any type of shooting. I hoped that, in time, he would find as much enjoyment in shooting flintlocks as I did.

Finally, I thought it might be time to introduce the children to black powder in a camp setting. The opportunity presented itself at a little gathering on our 40 acres, where we hosted eight other historical campers.

My good friend, Lawrence Howard, had brought along his son Caleb, who spent much of his time with John and Johannah. Lawrence had also brought a boy's rifle for his son to use in the competitions and mentored him as he loaded and shot the iron gongs set amid the shadows of the woods.

I could see my son wanted to shoot as well, which prompted me to work with him. At nearly seven years of age he was neither tall nor heavy, but he was eager. He shot my .54 caliber Virginia rifle with a reduced charge and he did admirably.

Then came Johannah, who watched all this and decided she was not going to let these boys have all the fun, so my spirited daughter, who was almost nine, also shot my rifle. She was a bit hesitant at first, but she also shot well.

Following that weekend, I began to consider when each child could handle a black powder firearm on their own and began to lament a missed opportunity to introduce them to Deerfoot. I could have shown it to them and told them of my history with it as well as the fact that their mother used it for her introduction to black powder muzzleloading. They were still young and I reminded myself there would be other opportunities. I considered retrieving it shortly after that, but I never got around to it. It remained stowed away still waiting to be relevant, waiting to be needed, waiting to be unwrapped, like some long forgotten mummy and assume its place as a necessary firearm.

As John grew, he asked more frequently about going hunting. I started him out with a small archery set and he followed behind me as I took him to areas where he might have an opportunity to take a snowshoe hare, but no opportunities were offered.

Several years later, during a warm spell in late in February he asked if he could try getting some game. We crawled to a small retaining wall and he loaded the .22 with my assistance. Thus deployed, he weeded out several pesky red squirrels around the house. I helped him skin them and we cooked them. With that short foray under his belt, he was excited at the thought of taking his first grey squirrel and ruffed grouse.

A short time later John and Johannah took their hunter safety classes together. Both passed with flying colors. I was one of two instructors that August and was pleased with both my children and the rest of the class. With attendance in that class successfully completed, those two received their own BB guns. Johannah's was pink, (of course) and after the class she seemed to "come of age" to handle guns.

She and her sister Sarah, would shoot their BB guns at the cans hung on strings in the back yard.

That first year, John bagged several grey squirrels and a grouse, all with a .410 shotgun. It was an exciting time for him.

In early 2009, I considered the upcoming rendezvous

season and I headed to the closet to get the old .45 rifle, but to my horror, I could not locate it. I sat there a bit befuddled and looked in a second place, but no rifle. I had searched for the better part of a day and had even gone back to the cabin where we lived prior to the new house. I searched and searched without success. Now I was becoming concerned.

I had indeed cleaned out the garage a bit the year before. Hopefully I had not mistakenly thrown it away. Could someone else have simply tossed it into the garbage, not knowing what was inside all of the bubble-wrap? I began to kick myself for not keeping better tabs on the piece. As the old saying goes, "out of sight, out of mind."

I had become wearied with searching, but before leaving the basement, I paused to lay back on the weight-lifting bench. I closed my eyes and began to think mighty hard. Had it really been over four years since I even handled the little .45 flinter? I let out a loud exasperated breath, and slowly, blankly panned across the area above me. Suddenly I focused on one of the items tucked in the open floor joists of the basement... Lo! There it was, in all of its wrapped-up-glory. I chuckled for quite a while before I retrieved it.

It took me quite a while to pull off the tape, plastic, bubble-wrap and rags until I had uncovered it in its entirety. A half an hour later, after cleaning it inside and out I brought it to the living room and showed my wife and children. It was a brief session, but it was important to me because the rifle was once again relevant.

The Surprise in Camp

Later in May, John and I were camping at a rendezvous near Kindred, North Dakota and, unbeknownst to him, I had brought along Deerfoot. I had a hunch that he might want to shoot that weekend, so I wanted to be ready.

On that same weekend, Lawrence Howard, was also in attendance, however this time he brought his younger son Isaac, who would be shooting his "boy's" rifle.

Mid-morning on Saturday, John wandered his way down to the shooting range where he saw Isaac, his friend and peer, busily engaged at the shooting range. Instead of wearing his usual smile, John seemed a bit downcast. After viewing my son's mood for a few minutes I thought a brief inquiry was in order. He was a bit depressed that he did not have a rifle of his own to shoot. At that point, I asked him if he was interested in shooting. His answer was an emphatic YES.

His elation, however, fizzled after he asked, *"Who's gun can I use?"*

I responded *"Let me worry about that. Stay put."* I walked away several paces and reached around a large white oak. What appeared in my hand was the slim .45 caliber longrifle that I had snuck from the tent only ten minutes before.

He was elated, but bewildered at the appearance of the gun. With knitted eyebrows, he observed, *"That looks like your rifle."*

I replied, *"It is my rifle."*

"How did it get here?" He asked incredulously.

"I brought it from home." I said. In the minute of silence that followed I considered that his inquiry was actually to himself, namely,

How could I have possibly missed the fact, that the rifle had been loaded into the car?

In any event, Deerfoot was again outside and ready for action. After a long, long, long absence, it was back in a

Looking Backward, Looking Forward

rendezvous camp and ready for a weekend of shooting.

This time the hands gripping the plain maple stock were those of an excited ten-year-old boy.

My own preparations for this event had begun a week or so before the camp, I had put together the basic contents to support the rifle in a shooting pouch such as a bag of .440 balls, short starter, vent pick[20], cloth for patching[21], turn-screw[22], powder horn, and a range rod[23] for the shooting line.

Now that we were at the shooting range for the rendezvous, I directed John to the loading tables behind the shooting lines and acquainted him with the rules of the range. I supervised his efforts while he focused on the loading process and let him work through the process without too much intervention.

He and I walked up to the shooting line where I picked out a likely tree to use as a brace. Since the rifle was a bit long (actually it was taller than John was, at the time), I helped him to support the rifle by planting my hand against a small tree. John used my wrist as a rest for the long barrel. He aimed and shot numerous times, hit some targets and felt pretty good about his performance. In between shots, as we walked between the loading tables and the shooting line, I asked him about his hold, the sights, reaching the trigger and a few more questions on how it felt to shoot.

The shooting line, as it turned out, was just a warm-up. Lawrence and I both chatted about other contests that day which prompted us to ask our respective sons whether they would like to compete as a four-person, father and son team in the "trail walk"[24] competition.

We were both allowed to help our sons and both boys shot well. John alone succeeded in hitting a "soldier" target at 175 yards when we three others did not. Towards the end of the walk, Lawrence and I helped to support Deerfoot for John by using two ramrods for a rest. John pivoted the rifle on them to follow a moving buffalo target, took aim and BOOM! He was rewarded by a quick PING!

"*He hit it!*" Lawrence and I exclaimed several times. I was so pleased with my son's eagerness to compete with Deerfoot, that I gifted to him my C.J. Wilde woven linen/wool tumpline, which he was borrowing as a sash. He still wears it as a sash to this day.

Several months later at another shoot, I was helping him load out of the pouch for some 25-yard practice targets when a news reporter took a photo (which ended up in the local paper). The image showed me, reclining on the ground with John, kneeling and shouldering the buttstock. The barrel of the rifle was laid across my raised knee.

I hoped that a thousand children might see that photo and in so doing, plant a seed of curiosity for historical shooting.

Though John was now shooting regularly, the next item we addressed before fall arrived, was a proper shooting pouch rather than the open-topped wool pouch he had been using.

I had picked up a commercial pouch from a widow whose husband had dabbled in muzzleloading. Perhaps it might fit the bill. The pouch needed some significant work, though, before it could be dependably used. It was made of flimsy under split cowhide, the closure of which was Velcro glued to the flap and body. The body was all-too shallow and tended to vomit out its contents. It would not stay closed even with the elongated flap which overlaid and hung very low. We both discussed the necessary changes needed to rehabilitate the pouch.

Looking Backward, Looking Forward

The first fix employed was: the body was deepened by adding a section of heavy, dark-brown, deer hide to the front which in turn shortened the front flap a bit. Then the corners of the taller section were pulled close to the body to keep the top more constricted. The strap was cut in half, and a buckle was added so that the strap could be lengthened as John grew. An inside pocket, against the back wall, (often called a ball-pocket) was also added to accommodate a "quick retrieve" area for balls or patching. A weeping heart cut-out, from the same dark deer hide, was used as a patch to cover the glue spot where the Velcro had been attached. With patience and careful sewing, the structural flaws were addressed. I added a powder measure (for a .45 caliber charge) made from a deer antler.

As for the tools I assembled: a forged turn-screw, three-cornered file, .45 caliber jag, and vent pick all of which were kept in a cloth pouch. I also helped him make a new ball bag, with an antler spout, and *viola*! the pouch was ready for some serious use.

That fall and winter I took John out to hunt with the rifle. In the back of my sash was tucked a set of cross sticks made of 3/4 inch dowels tied to create bi-pod. This set up provided a steady rest. During these forays we discussed the different hunting strategies for many types of game, including squirrels, grouse, rabbits, woodchucks, porcupine, and deer.

At that time I discussed putting his sights on a bear and whether he would be able to see his front sight; made of iron. I suggested that he put his sights on a dark spot of a tree to see if his sights were discernable. He agreed that they were a bit hard to see because the front sight was dull and rust-colored. With that I showed him how use a file to shine up the back edge of the iron front sight so it would show up in the shade of the forest and provide a contrast against the dark fur of his quarry. With this tip he regularly kept the front sight shiny.

The following spring, the rifle again accompanied John as we attended various rendezvous camps, where he used it to compete in shooting contests.

Into the next fall, it again accompanied us along with the cross sticks. On these forays, we took time to pause and review different scenarios in which I would deploy the crossed sticks and he quietly, but quickly, placed Deerfoot in the crotch of the sticks followed by acquiring a mock target; as if it were a deer. As long as it shot straight, he could take his first deer with it.

At the end of the deer season, however, I could tell that he was troubled about shooting the rifle, so I provoked a conversation about his reticence.

It seemed that in the interim year, he had seen a number of frontier movies in which the "old guns" were portrayed to kick like a mule. He confessed watching the guns being shot had created some anxiety. After all, the guns being shot were real, therefore the recoil must also be real.

I replied that Hollywood made it look as though the "old guns," meaning muzzleloaders, delivered a *hard recoil!* But the reality is, even when loaded with a deer hunting charge, they do not have a sharp recoil; rather they push. I made sure he understood the scenes he had been watching were just movie stunts.

I went on to tell him that the modern cartridge guns like his .410 and 20 gauge, actually have greater recoil due to the modern powder used. Further, we do not use modern powder in muzzleloaders; instead, we use only real black powder. More to the point, the charges we use are moderate. We have no need for big charges which are wasteful of powder and often hamper accuracy.

I then gave him a rule: *"Let the gun do its work; let it push you and do not flinch when you pull the trigger."* As the afternoon light began to wane, I had him load and shoot the rifle several times and reminded him of the rule. Sure enough, he realized the recoil from black powder was minimal at best, and in his countenance, I saw him relax. It seemed as though the anxiety had been replaced by trust in my words and confidence in himself. The tension in his face began to dissipate by degrees until a subtle grin broke into a full smile. Now, he spoke about wanting to shoot it more.

With the arrival of summer, he was strong enough to hold the rifle on his own and the more he shot it, the more confident he became with it.

Later, in anticipation of the upcoming hunting season, I showed John a pattern for a lock cover. After retrieving a section of dark deer hide, I helped John to trace out, cut and sew his own lock-cover; which he completed fairly quickly. Following that, I showed him the proper way to apply it to the breech area of the rifle. When it was not in use, it should remain rolled up and tucked away in his hunting pouch until needed for inclement weather.

That fall he succeeded in taking his first flintlock grey squirrel with the rifle, off hand, without the use of any brace. It was a thirty yard shot, and he hit the squirrel cleanly, dropping it to the ground. He was, needless to say, becoming quite handy with the trim flintlock.

During that regular deer season, he and Johannah came out with me to the blind, during several day-trips. John also spent a lot of time with me stalking the woods as well as in the deer blind and deer stand, but he wasn't able to connect with his modern cartridge gun.

For muzzleloading season, Deerfoot was his "go-to" rifle and he wielded it firmly like a good rifleman. As the end of muzzleloading season drew near, however, John was facing the prospect that he might not shoot a deer that year. He had many opportunities to shoot during both seasons, but something always stood in the way of a *clear* shot. Before we knew it, the last weekend of the muzzleloader season had arrived. My admonishment to him was, "It's time to get serious."

His response, though subdued was, "I agree."

Looking Backward, Looking Forward

Top-Author's son taking his first shots at the Rendezvous near Kindred ND. Bottom-Author's son taking aim on a long distance target at Kindred. Photo courtesy of Monte Mertz.

Top-Author coaching his son - while seating a ball at the muzzle - during the Trail Walk at Kindred, ND. Photo courtesy of Monty Mertz.
Bottom-During the trail walk, author mentoring son on the basics of flintlock ignitions, and keeping the touch hole clear. Far left is Lawrence Howard, In the white shirt and tricorn hat is Howard's son Isaac. Photo Courtesy Monty Mertz.

Looking Backward, Looking Forward

Top-Author's daughter, Johannah, practicing basic muzzleloading using a plastic polymer range rod. Bottom-Johannah, trying her hand at the cross sticks in a low profile and giving her brother John some competition with Deerfoot.

Top-John practicing with Deerfoot using different positions on the cross sticks. The remodeled pouch hangs at his side.
Bottom-John with a satisfied grin after taking a squirrel at 30 yards, using Deerfoot off-hand, and no cross sticks.

Chapter 13
The First Time to Go-It Alone

We both got to the woods early that Saturday morning. I put John in the stand and I went to a nearby ridge within eyesight of him. It was an uncomfortably cold, damp, frosty morning and we were ready for a warm-up by 10:30 a.m. However, before we headed out of the woods, I felt that we should relocate the deer stand because it seemed too exposed, and the sitter was too easily seen by the deer.

We quietly and methodically unhooked and lowered the ladder and walked it to a clump of basswoods twenty-five yards further to the west. It was nearer to one brushy trail and better hidden from a nearby opening. The clump of trees would be good cover to break up his outline, provide a good surround for security, and afford him places to hang his pack and other stuff. Most importantly, he could hang the rifle on a type of hook that I had invented. With everything ready to go, we left for lunch.

We returned at about 2:00 p.m. with a simple plan for me to work on a one-man drive or rather, a gentle push. I reviewed a number of scenarios with him related to shooting, and loading. I stressed that if he needed to, he could climb down the ladder and reload on the ground. I had also, by that time, taught him how to load without the use of a short starter. This time saving short-cut also seemed to give him confidence.

He had taken his very first deer the year before using a modern gun with me at his side. This year would prove to be a different scenario altogether. He would be by himself to "go-it alone." In order to take his second deer in two years, he would have to shoot it with a flintlock muzzleloader; one with which he was familiar from several years of shooting at rendezvous and small game.

I told him several times, *"You can do this."* Some of the last-minute details I checked were; to make sure the flint was clamped securely in the jaws of the cock, and that it held a keen edge.

I said a quick prayer, gave him a hug and had him climb the ladder. I then handed Deerfoot up to him. Upon my suggestion, he raised it to his shoulder to aim at several marks out around him. He told me he felt stable, balanced and confident. I asked him, *"What are you going to aim for?"*

He replied, *"I'm gonna shoot for one hair,"* he paused for a second, grinned and then added, *"Aim small, miss small."*

I looked up at him with a grin and nodded back. He would be alone here for over an hour while I walked east on the road ¾ of a mile, then south a ¼ mile, and then westerly on another road ¾ of a mile before I could even begin to the drive to him.

After 45 minutes of walking and a ten-minute rest stop to shed a layer, I entered the woods again. As I slipped through the trees, the wind was at my back, and thus it would be in his face. The day was a cool 28 degrees with some patches of snow on the ground imprinted with fresh tracks.

I eased along slowly and within ten minutes, jumped several deer. I paused to listen and could hear a number of them, but could only see two tails. I kept my pace slow and steady. Rather than crest a ridge, where I would be silhouetted, I picked my way through the brush in order to

The First Time to Go-It Alone

dip down into the edge of a grassy pond. I wanted the deer to hear me, but not see me. I wanted to bump them into moving, not pressure them into high-speed flight.

All was quiet. I stalked up towards the next ridge and as I came to a cross-trail I heard the sharp *crack* of a rifle. I prayed at that moment that all was well, and that the shot was fired straight to kill a deer. I walked through the woods and tangles of brush until I came to familiar trail.

The day was getting long and I knew if he had hit a deer, we would need all the light possible, so I wasted no time in following that trail to another that led right to him. As I approached him on the rather thin ribbon of a toe-path threading its way amongst the pine, maple and raspberry, I had to step up and over a blown down tree and then ascend a small rise to reach higher ground. Finally, I could see the orange rabbit fur hat on John's head. He was searching back and forth for my appearance.

As soon as he caught a glimpse of me, he excitedly waved me on. He had indeed shot at a deer, a big doe. He showed me the hair on the ground. Initially I had him stay in the stand to direct me and tell me how the encounter played out. Eventually, I had him climb down, and we both moved in half circles, searching in the thick brush. After what seemed to me like an eternity, but in reality was only about three to four minutes, I found the doe. She was dead a mere 30 yards from the spot where she had been standing when he shot her. The linen-patched .440 home-molded, round ball had found its mark in the heart-lung area. The lead ball had broken a rib upon entering, and broken another upon exiting.

Off in the distance, I could see at least one if not two other deer. No doubt, it was the group that had come through with the doe. I considered another shot at a deer and called out with a deer bleat to entice at least one of them closer. Time however, was not on our side. The waning light of day made me feel a bit rushed for that endeavor and, in my discretion, I decided that this day belonged to John Spencer and Deerfoot. I got his attention by whistling out with a loon call. With a slow hand gesture, I motioned for him to head my way.

He called out, *"Did you find her?"*

I gave him a thumbs-up followed by a finger to my lips for him to not talk.

When he stood only a few feet away, he asked in a hushed tone, *"Where is she?"*

I stepped back to hold down some brush. He stepped forward and when he saw her on the ground he replied, *"Yes, thank you, Lord."* He gave me a hug and asked where he had hit her.

"You hit her in the heart lung, buddy. Nice job," I said, confirming what he thought had been his point of aim.

At that point I asked him to recount how the situation had played out for him. He began by telling me that he saw the deer approaching from a low area to his left. As soon as he saw them he unhooked Deerfoot and brought it to his right side. The lock cover was in place, so this was pulled off to one side and out of the way.

He kept his eye on the closest deer (which was a big doe) walking along a somewhat cluttered trail. As he was anticipating a shot on the doe, she stopped behind a large pine tree, blocking any chance of a shot. John then directed his attention at the spike to his far left. It was looking in his direction quite intently and John hoped it had not spotted him. If the spike was going to be the one deer to spook, John thought he would shoot him, because all the other deer were either obscured by brush and, except for the doe, the others were smaller.

As the spike began to feed and look elsewhere, the doe began to move from behind the tree and past some brush. John realized at that moment his best and closest opportunity for the biggest deer in the group was the doe. He slowly raised the gun to his shoulder while keeping an eye on her. As the rifle butt came to rest on his shoulder he could see in his periphery that the spike was focused on his stand. Sensing that he did not have much time, he located a hole in the brush that would admit a shot and brought the lock to full cock.

As John brought the barrel of Deerfoot to bear, the doe took another step into a better opening in the brush. He moved the barrel until the sights were at the heart/lung area on the doe. He quickly set the back trigger and reached for the front trigger. Within a second or two he touched the front trigger and the gun cracked out its shot. He looked through the cloud of smoke to see where the doe bolted into the brush, but his vision was obscured. He sat very still to see if he could hear anything.

He could feel his heart pounding and knew he had to reload so he climbed down to the ground, reloaded, and then stood there for a moment before climbing back into the stand for a better view. He primed the pan, and while standing up there, he could see what looked like a patch of hair. A few minutes later he dumped his prime, climbed down and confirmed it was a patch of hair cut by the shot.

He felt like combing the area for sign and stepped out about eight or ten more steps to locate some blood, but stopped. He wanted to wait for me so he climbed back into the stand. A few minutes later he spotted me as I came onto the scene. As he finished recounting his experience, I complimented him on a job well done.

It was his first muzzleloader deer. Though 21 years had spanned our respective accomplishments, he had used the same rifle that I had used to take my first muzzleloader deer. I stood there as he unsheathed his belt knife with its heavily figured maple scales. It was a knife he and I had made by cutting down a larger butcher knife into the shape of a common trade knife. As he gutted and cleaned the big doe, I kept my eye on the spot where the other deer were milling around. I told him about them and suggested that if they came closer, I would give him first crack. He showed me his bloody hands as if to say that Deerfoot would get messy. My response was that any blood could be washed off when he got back home. He nodded at the thought that he might get another shot. I assured him I would back him up, but the deer kept their distance.

With the gutting done, we saved the heart and liver, and bagged them. John made a slit in the hock and attached his tag, after which, I also wrapped a length of cloth around hock to cover and protect the tag from being torn off in the brush.

He walked over to the base of a tree, and cleaned his knife blade and handle on the snow covered moss as he had seen me do a number of times. With water from my canteen dribbled onto the blade and handle, he wiped it with a rag from his pack and re sheathed the blade.

I obtained from my pack a hempen drag rope which I had made specifically for this purpose. I showed him how to bring the front legs over the neck and cross them behind the head; then secure the front legs, head and neck, with the

The First Time to Go-It Alone

drag rope. My next move was to pull the rope up to my waist to tow the deer.

With light fading fast, I took the lead dragging the doe and he followed me clutching Deerfoot in his right hand and my Virginia rifle in his left.

We changed our direction in the thick under brush at least a dozen times. Back and forth we trudged to find the barely discernible connecting trails and the "paths of least resistance." At one point he asked if he could drag the doe. My response alluded to the fact that the doe was as heavy "dressed" as he was wringing wet. He simply nodded and continued to clutch both rifles, but I could tell he really wanted to drag his own deer. I knew the trail in the day time, but there was a heavy cloud cover, absolutely zero moonlight and with full dark nearly upon us, I had to get within six inches of several blazes to double check the trail. We really needed to keep on moving, or we would be fumbling around in the dark woods.

At length, we reached an open glade separating us from our long sought destination namely, the road. After a small pause from the laborious drag, we pressed on through the rather open glade and up to the grassy right of way. I shucked the drag rope from my waist, took my rifle in hand and walked down the road, to retrieve the car.

In the meantime John Spencer, had pulled up the drag rope to his waist and, with Deerfoot in hand, dragged the doe a full fifty yards further along the right of way, before I returned with the car. Apparently dragging his doe was something he felt he really needed to do, and even though he was of slight build at that time, he more than made up for it in his determination.

As I was driving back I realized that he was quite a

ways from the trail and actually had found a more open, grassy parcel of right-of-way which was perfect for photos.

By the time we were able to take photos, it was just plain dark. I had to set the timer on the camera and place it on a stable surface so it would be free of vibrations from me holding it. A few photos were taken (as best we could), after which the doe was loaded and brought home to hang in the garage. We weighed her and she tipped the scales at 125 pounds dressed, a nice deer! That evening not only marked the end of a successful deer season, but a milestone in the history of Deerfoot.

Both John and I were pretty sweated up, so we each hit the shower and got cleaned up before supper. We were both ready for some hot food.

Connie had been preparing her homemade pizza, and by the time John and I were sitting at the table, she and Johannah had everything ready for the meal.

While we ate, John talked about the hunt from his perspective. In like manner, I related my part of the hunt as well followed by a handful of questions from Connie and Johannah.

It had been a grand day in the north woods. That night we all, especially John, slept soundly, thankful for the harvest blessings.

The First Time to Go-It Alone

John sitting atop the ladder stand in its new location. After strapping a tree-hook to the tree, he is hanging his pack from it within easy reach of the stand, and preparing for the hunt.

Basswood trees, which often grow in a clump, were useful in breaking up John's outline in the rather open pine canopy.

Deerfoot hangs, barrel down, from a second hook also within easy reach.

The fruits of a long day, good planning and confidence behind the gun. The .440 home molded, round ball killed cleanly and quickly. The lock cover - unfurled over the comb - can be seen on the rifle, just behind the lock area.

My Journey with Deerfoot

John's first flintlock deer hanging in the garage just after the hunt. The rather large doe tipped the scales at over 125 lbs. John wears clothing of the same cut and style as 18th century clothing, the style which is most often worn while shooting the flintlocks, especially at primitive camps and rendezvous.

Chapter 14
Revelations from an Old Barrel

The next year I put a new silver front sight on the barrel in an effort to dispense with shining up the iron one I had originally installed. But, try as I may, the rifle would not group consistently. The shots were hitting in one of five different places on the target. I might get three hits in the upper left and then one or two down in the lower left followed by a shot to the middle and then several more just below and to the right of center. The next shot would be back up in the upper left and then two to the upper right. The only thing consistent about the shots is that all shots hit within an inch or so of these five places. I swabbed and loaded and shot in three round groups but to no avail. Therefore, after expending thirty shots or more, on target, I came to the realization that the bore was "washed out." My next move was to determine the cost of a replacement barrel.

I resolved that the old 13/16 barrel would be pulled off the rifle when I ordered the new one. As for the old barrel I did not discard it because I might use it for some project; I just did not know what that might be. That question would be answered, however several months later in February when I traveled down to a Contemporary Longrifle Association (CLA) show on Lake Cumberland near Jamestown, Kentucky.

My reason for being there was to attend a trade fair put on by Mel Hankla, The show itself was started and managed by Mel, to host talented artisans within the CLA, and create a venue to display, buy and sell.

As I perused numerous goods and collections, I spied an interesting antique barrel on a table, which had a nice looking pipe bowl forged into the end. The intent was most likely a gun-barrel pipe-tomahawk because an eye had also been forged next to the pipe bowl. At that moment, I envisioned at least two or three tomahawk heads with my old barrel. Following that, there might even be enough left over to make a pistol barrel. Though any pistol barrel would need to be sleeved and re-rifled, my effort to re purpose the barrel for several projects was taking shape. I would be able to continue the legacy of the rifle. It had come full circle from me to my son to make meat in the forest, and continued to provide for us as the tradition was passed down to the next generation.

Six months later, while attending the CLA convention in Lexington, KY, I spoke with Jason Schneider from Rice Barrel Company, in order to get my name on the waiting list for a new barrel.

In 2014, I pulled the old barrel off of the stock and removed the breech plug as Jason had suggested and sent it with my payment. By sending the old breech plug the threads could be matched in pitch and length and the plug installed there in the shop.

A month later, I called Jason to ask where the barrel was and a day after that he called back saying it had been sent well over two weeks earlier. When I quizzed my son, John whether a long round tube had been delivered by UPS from North Carolina his reply was silence, followed by,

"Oh yeah, I think I put it into your office closet."

Sure enough there it was. I cut open the tube and removed a bright, shiny, new .45 caliber barrel. It was 42 inches long, and rifled with seven round-bottomed riflings, and had the breech plug installed. I made a quick call back to Jason to assure him all was well.

Revelations from an Old Barrel

I had all the intentions of getting to the barrel within the next several weeks, but as usual, other chores took precedence. At least ten months passed before I finally tended to my project. I spent several evenings preparing the barrel by filing dove-tails for three loops [25] into which pins would be inserted. I sawed off one inch from the muzzle, to fit the slightly shorter stock. Following that, I filed down the sharp edges into single facets around the muzzle and re-crowned inside of face of the bore. I blued the barrel, after which I filed in two more dove tails; one for the new front sight and the other for the old rear sight.

At long last it was set into the stock with the breech plug nestling right back into its original mortise. I pinned the barrel to the stock, followed by drilling the touch hole with a 5/64 drill bit. The hole was oriented just above the "horizon" of the lock pan and centered over the "dish" of the pan. Finally, it was ready for shooting.

I hastily trotted outside, into the yard, where I loaded and shot it at least ten times. The charges ignited well with both FFg and FFFg. I swabbed it out and examined the cleaning patches to look for cuts and found none. I shot it another ten or so times and swabbed it as before.

Thereafter, I spent the next several days sighting in the gun and, in all honesty, getting reacquainted with an old friend. The result of all that work and preparation made me eager to get out in the woods and bag some squirrels.

My next endeavor, therefore, was to make a new shooting bag just for the rifle. Though my son already had a pouch set up for .45 caliber, I needed to have *my own* shooting pouch with a powder horn to support the rifle.

I recalled having obtained a number of raw horns from well-known horner Lee Larkin. He had sold to me a half dozen creamy-white horns with dark, charcoal tips for that classic look. I searched my box of trade goods and found one that I had made the year prior. For some reason, it had not sold, even after being displayed on the blanket at several camps, and a price tag of $45.00. There was a reason, however, it had not sold. It seems my own needs would be better served by using it with a new bag.

    The bag I made was nothing fancy, just practical. Its lines follow the fashion of bags from the late eighteenth and early nineteenth centuries. It was composed of thinner, bark tanned deer on the outside and inside a mahogany colored layer of commercial tanned deer (from the smallest deer I ever shot). In addition to the welted seams, I inserted a bottom gusset to enlarge the bottom of the bag. The addition of this gusset allowed the upper portion of the bag to remain flat by keeping the contents seated at the bottom instead of bulging out in the middle like a pot belly. Also, a "ball pocket" was sewn against the back wall.

    The strap, from C.J. Wilde, runs for two thirds of its length with a dark color for the weft, then white for the last third. I believe her intention was probably to use up her remnants of woolen yarn by using plain white to finish the strap.

    Once I saw it, I had to have it. It is a metaphor that speaks to the desire of a crafts person to "finish the job." In this case, the strap is not only functional, but with two colors it is more interesting. When I sewed the strap in place I made sure its orientation on the bag echoed the white butt and black spout of the horn.

    As for accoutrements, my first addition to the pouch was a powder measure made from a hollowed out deer antler. The next addition was a bag for the round balls. The little bag, fashioned from bark-tanned deer hide, would have a short length of antler with one end being the crown or rosette (from the pedicel on the skull). The crown would be inside, covered by the top of the ball-bag, and sewn in place to form a hard spout. I braided a tether as an attachment to the shooting bag strap. This type of ball-bag was identical to the first one I made when I started my black powder career.

As I began to gather tools, I recalled earlier in the winter, while at the CLA show in Lake Cumberland, I had obtained a high-quality, forged turn-screw from Rich McDonald. It was a welcomed addition.

My next purchase occurred while attending the Spring Trade Faire at Ft. Des Chartres in Illinois. I headed to see Larry Callahan where I gladly parted with the money necessary to obtain a new .440 bag mold, to stay with the pouch. As with my other pouches, a small three-cornered file was included as well. The last necessities were strips of patching, round balls, flints and powder for the horn.

I have had many forays into the woods with the rifle and new pouch and used them to take squirrels and small game.

Often times hobbies, crafts and avocations provide an opportunity to explore a number of different things and in so doing, discover what we do not want. That knowledge allows us to focus on the one thing that we do want.

With that in mind, one of the changes I made to the new pouch, was to switch out the first ball bag I had made. In its place, I fashioned a typical flat, onion shaped ball bag that opens by pinching the seams together. Even though the deer antler-spout bag was nostalgic, I had grown used to fifteen years of using the pinch type bag; which conveniently sits in the "ball pocket" at the back wall of the pouch. The new bag, following this slight amendment, supports Deerfoot superbly.

Looking back on its history: I am glad for all the starts, and stops, the victories and failures, mistakes and repairs, problems and revelations. I am blessed with my gift of persevering when others were telling me to quit and take the "easy route." I am also thankful that I was able to pass down the tradition, history and practical use of flintlock that is relevant 35 years later and still counting. My journey with Deerfoot has been and continues to be part of a fulfilling pastime with firearms.

The fact is, that plain, humble rifle became the catalyst for a life-long study of the American Colonial culture. It has been an adventure of discovery; an extensive journey that lead me to the love of flintlocks in general, and the continuing desire to unravel more historical traditions - as yet undiscovered - that adhere to their use.

Revelations from an Old Barrel

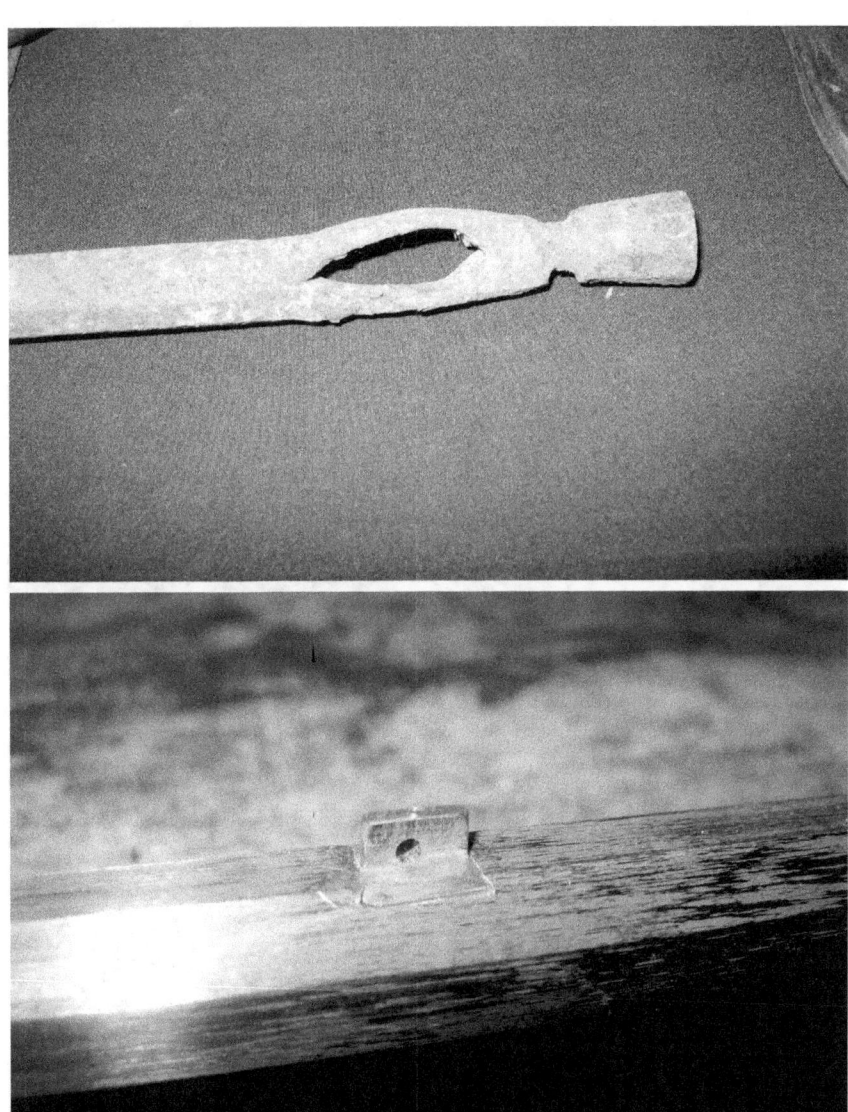

Top-On display at the CLA, Lake Cumberland, KY trade show, an old barrel with the makings of a pipe bowl and eyelet for a handle forged into one end.

Bottom-A loop, inserted into a dovetail on the bottom of the barrel. The loop fits into a mortise cut into the barrel channel of the stock. A hole is drilled to accommodate a pin which secures the stock to the barrel. This barrel has three loop/pin attachments, as well as two screws that secure the tang at the wrist.

Top-The original rear sight, removed from the first barrel and re-installed on the new barrel. Sighting-in is accomplished by *gently* hammering the rear sight to the left or right in the same direction as needed to move the hits on the target.

Bottom-The new German silver front sight installed. Silver shows up in the dark forest or against the dark fur of a game animal. Elevation is raised by filing the front sight to a lower profile. Elevation can be lowered by filing the rear sight to a lower profile. Both sights are installed using dovetails in a tight friction fit.

Revelations from an Old Barrel

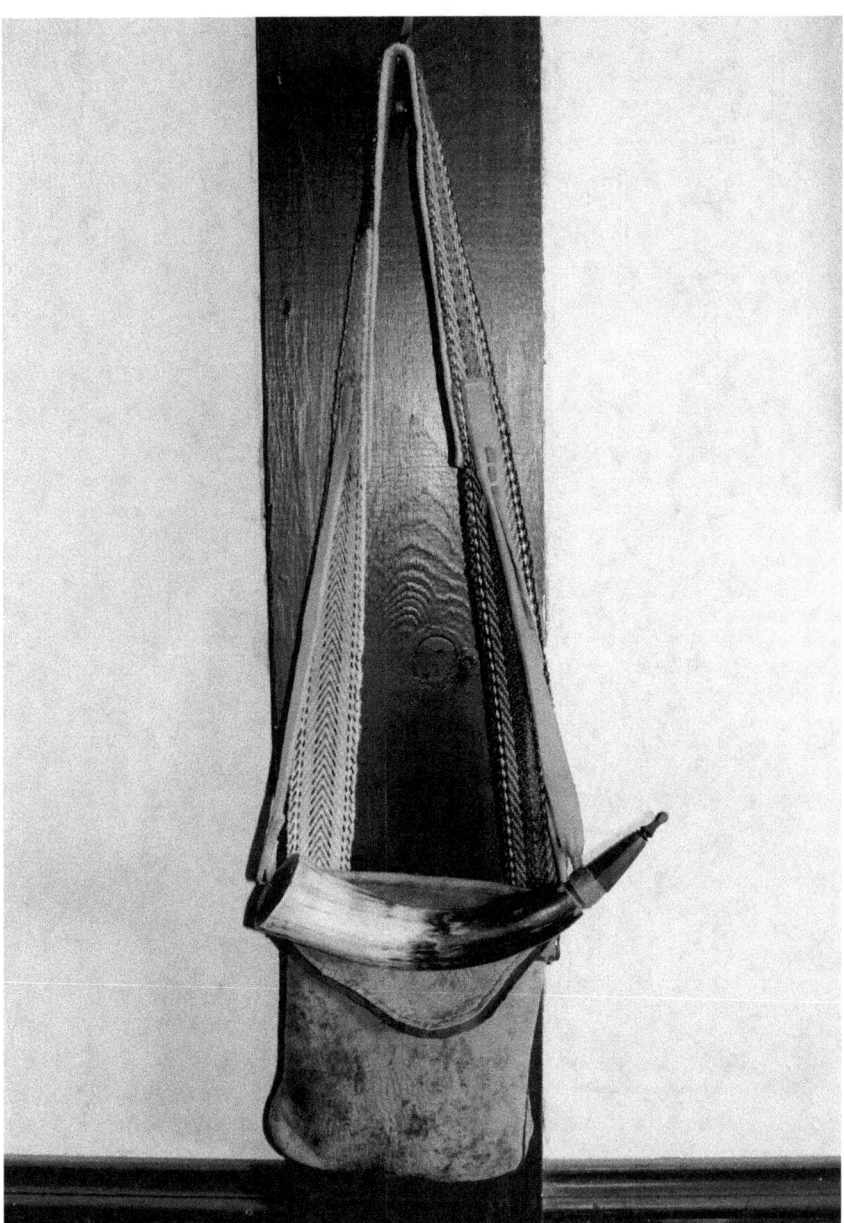

The new pouch for Deerfoot, made from bark tan outside and a mahogany colored commercial tan inside. Notice the C.J. Wilde shoulder strap echoes the light and dark of the horn. The raw horn was purchased from Lee Larkin and the author fashioned it with a pine butt and staple for the strap. The front strap fits in a recess behind the octagon facette of the spout. A violin key provides the plug.

Top-Bullet bag for the .440 round balls which is opened by squeezing the outer seams together. It closes by flattening. The body is made of heavy deer hide, the upper pieces are of buffalo.

Bottom left-The "ball pocket" against the back wall of the pouch holds the ball pouch. As the ball pouch is placed in the ball pocket it is held at the top which pinches the opening flat again.

Bottom right-The gusset at the bottom of the pouch allows the pouch to swell at the bottom instead of mid-body. The contents remain toward the bottom, giving the bag a flatter profile.

Chapter 15
The Legacy Continues

I thought long and hard on the subject of cutting up the old barrel from Deerfoot and remaking it into a number of items. First on the list was my son's suggestion that I save the breech end for a pistol barrel of fourteen inches or so. That would leave me with roughly twenty-seven inches of barrel that I could cut into four pieces and use those to make gun-barrel tomahawks.

The second item, or rather question was, who was going to make the tomahawks? Sure, I could cut the barrel up with the intention of using the four short pieces for some form of tomahawk, but before I did any cutting, I had to know the proper amount of material with which to start. Would six and three quarters of an inch be sufficient for each tomahawk? Moreover, should I cut up the barrel at all?

The more I analyzed the intended project, the more questions I had, which could only be answered by someone with experience in these matters. I would have to bend the ear of a blacksmith, or blade smith.

I began to look at the artisans who made beautiful pipe tomahawks from gun barrels, including a steel bit forged into the head. The prices ranged from $400.00 for a single head with a solid poll to as much as $900.00 base price for a finished "smoke-able" pipe tomahawk. However, in order to obtain a finely polished, engraved head, hafted with a heavily tiger-striped maple handle, the asking prices started in the $1,200.00 to $1,400.00 range and up.

I was a stunned. The last tomahawk with a poll that I had purchased, in 1990, cost $45.00, and was hafted with a plain hickory handle (see page 120 supra). It was made

My Journey with Deerfoot

by Keith Johnson who operated Great River Forge; prior to selling his business, he produced literally several thousand tomahawks. With the sale of his business, it was doubtful whether he could help in my new endeavor.

My next option included viewing a DVD of famed Colonial Williamsburg gunsmith, Wallace Gusler forging a punched eye, pipe tomahawk hafted with a maple handle and was smoke-able.[26] Though I have a forge, I am no blacksmith. I have made a few items by pounding hot iron, but as a rule I have not forge-welded. I watched the DVD several times; especially the portion on forge-welding a high carbon bit into the front of the wrought iron body of the tomahawk. Wallace makes it looks so easy. After viewing it numerous times, I thought, maybe I should try to forge one tomahawk by my own hand; but thinking about it and doing it are two entirely different things.

It was at this point that I began to feel rather silly about the whole endeavor. After all, the old barrel had been replaced by a new one and I should just let go of the inclination to hold onto that old barrel.

Though the thought of a pipe tomahawk was intriguing, there is one thing I did not need; namely, the time commitment to a project outside my usual skill set. After much rumination, I resolved not to abandon the project, because it seemed rooted in history. I had heard the term gun-barrel-pipe tomahawk too many times to ignore it, but I had a dilemma. Could I find and employ another to make a tomahawk for me?

One day I called down to Kentucky to touch base with well-known master gunsmith Mike Miller. We conferred about the Tennessee rifle, its history and origins. During the call he mentioned Simeon England, an accomplished blacksmith and tomahawk maker, who had recently moved down to Edmonton, Kentucky. He lived a mere six miles from Mike. This was good news indeed, because I had tried, unsuccessfully, to reach Simeon about nine months earlier. I knew Simeon made tomahawks, good ones! I had handled his pieces two years earlier. Moreover, I had seen photos of his more recent pieces, including several more selections in styles, and had been hearing good comments about them. I told Mike that I had not made contact with Simeon for almost a year and the next thing I knew, I had a message waiting from none other than...Simeon himself.

    I had several phone conversations with Simeon in which we discussed his work at the forge, the influence of his earlier gunsmithing efforts on tomahawk production, and his research. When I asked about gun barrels specifically, he quickly related that, gunsmiths were in fact the most apt to forge a tomahawk from a gun barrel. They usually had a ready supply of old, used and damaged gun barrels with which to work. Upon choosing a barrel, the end intended for the re purposed project would be cleaned up and then inserted into the forge to begin working. The barrel would be left whole and more efficiently worked by holding the cold end. When I heard those words, I was thankful that I had not cut the barrel into separate pieces.

    As an artisan, Simeon has dedicated many hundreds of hours to blacksmithing and especially forging and finishing tomahawks. He has acquired his proficiency by working hard and also tapping the knowledge of none other than, Wallace Gusler himself. In pursuit of his smithing endeavors, Simeon dedicated several weeks to forging tomahawks by traveling to Wallace's house in Williamsburg, Virginia and working at the forge there with Wallace.

Following that, Simeon industriously turned out a steady supply of tomahawks. Since that trip, Simeon has made several refinements which have turned out to be real time savers.

The basic steps of making any punched eye tomahawk are: forging to shape, forge-welding the bit, punching the eye and forming the basic bowl shape. Following that, different files are used to "hog-off" unwanted material and clean up all the surfaces to remove the forging marks. The inside of the eye is filed relative to the blade, so the handle (once inserted) will index with the cutting-edge. It is also done to evenly maintain the general wall thickness of the eye as well as assure maximum surface contact between the inside of the eye and the handle.

Filing may be used to round out the pipe bowl or to develop facets or both. Filing is further used to fine tune the symmetry and subtly develop multiple planes of architecture. It has often been said that the most common sound heard from a gunsmith's shop was that of filing. Every metal part that went into a rifle, smoothbore or, in this case, a tomahawk, met with the file. The file was used to give the final shape to the forged and cast parts. When the filing is done the head is hardened, followed by tempering. Then, comes the polishing, engraving, and preparation for inlays.

The term "pipe tomahawk" can be defined by many different grades. Also, a pipe tomahawk made from a gun barrel will, in all likelihood, have a rounded pipe bowl rim and contoured facets that diminish into the constricted throat of the pipe bowl. Thus, the pipe may have no facets at all which echo the octagonal barrel from whence it came. Therefore, just because it came from a gun barrel, does not mean it has to look like a gun barrel.

The Legacy Continues

During one discussion, I mentioned that even though I had never forge welded, I should try to forge at least one tomahawk. Following a lengthy silence, Simeon calmly admonished me that for someone who has not done any forge-welding, making a tomahawk is fairly advanced and is not the place to learn how to forge-weld. He likened it to a young shop student with scant forge experience trying to forge a twenty-eight-inch sword blade. His comparison was not lost on me. Making a durable long-sword is the epitome of blade making. So too, punched-eye tomahawks are the ultimate combination of welding, symmetrical shaping and drawing out the poll end, but in the case of a gun barrel pipe tomahawk, with finer, proportions, lighter weight and more graceful esthetics. This project, in reality, was way outside of my skill set. If I wanted it done right the first time, I should allow a master to do it.

For my part, I was not looking for anything overly fancy. In fact, I was not looking for anything that was even polished or smooth. I would be satisfied with forge marks being left in the piece. I was most concerned that the weld for the hardened bit took hold without any cold-shuts or delaminations.

Perhaps Simeon would be willing to indulge me and, in the process, I could watch him at work. He has taken the gift for metal smithing and honed it into the skill of a professional, which would be a treat to watch.

In the final analysis I was also reconciled to the fact that Simeon was the artisan/smith who would either take on this project or decline it. He had offered several choices for his work. I understood that if his name were associated with this, I would have to accept what *he* wanted to do. Simeon sells his tomahawks "ready to use." He does not ship out anything half-done; therefore, he commented, "I finish the product or I don't sign it." My tomahawk, therefore, would not be rough forged, but tempered, polished, and hafted as a finished piece.

A Trip to Kentucky

In the Spring of 2022, I headed down to Edmonton Kentucky, arriving there Monday evening, and spent two days plus with Simeon at his home. He showed me a number of his pieces which I handled and studied. They were light, and quick to swing. Simeon made sure we watched several informative videos, in his collection, on tomahawks and their history. He also provided a number of excerpts from historic journals referencing axes, tomahawks and the like.

I had brought the old barrel from Deerfoot and showed him what I had in mind. Early on Tuesday morning the first thing I did was to make coffee in my copper camp kettle. While I was busy with that, Simeon made breakfast for the both of us, but he is a tea drinker, so I had the coffee all to myself, besides, he used a drip coffee maker to brew his tea, and did not want any coffee in it to ruin the taste of his tea.

After breakfast he started forging the tomahawk with the old barrel, while I took a collection of photographs. It took most of the day, but by three o'clock he was filing off the forging marks. He would end up keeping this one in his shop however. There was something odd, though, about the consistency of the steel at the end of the barrel; as it developed surface-tension cracks. However, the area of the eye, the pipe bowl and stem, which are prone to greater stress, had no cracks what-so-ever. I took several photos of that first-off tomahawk head in its filed state and we called it a day.

The Legacy Continues

Simeon would go on to forge a second head a short time later, but with no cracks or flaws in it. It gave me a sense of accomplishment finally seeing the head in its finished state.

Through his efforts, I had finally made a connection with a historical process that commonly re purposed barrels into works of beauty and functionality, but most importantly Simeon's work would continue the legacy of Deerfoot.

In an interesting side note...

Simeon suggested the best way to get used to the forge-welding process is to weld chain links, lots of them! Chains in the eighteenth century were forge welded with the lap-joint of the weld being at one end and each side of the lap had a slight curve to match the shape of the link. First a number of single links are forged to shape and welded shut. Next, two of them are connected by an adjoining link in the middle which is then welded shut. Thereafter, short three-link lengths are connected by inserting a link between them. By forging dozens, if not hundreds of chain links, an apprenticing smith becomes used to the color of hot iron when it is ready to "take a weld."

Part and parcel of welding in this manner is the feel of the soft, hot iron under the hammer. A hammer blow that is too heavy will push the weldable metal out the side and make for a poor weld or none at all. When hot iron oxidizes it produces a thin film of scale; iron will not weld through scale. Therefore, in order to impede the development of scale, borax is used to flux the hot surface and while it is still bubbling on the surface, the pieces of iron are struck together. It is not a hard strike, but just enough to blend the two pieces into one.

My Journey with Deerfoot

I have no illusions of being a chain maker, but I would be willing to try to make a six-foot chain. I will probably ruin a number of links in the process, but if successful, I could use it to hold my 12-gallon trade-kettle for boiling down maple sap into syrup.

I spoke to Wallace Gusler a few years earlier about welding with flux in the 18th century. He stated even though borax alone will work as a flux, smiths would often incorporate iron filings and sand mixed with borax. He did not give me any proportions though and perhaps that was bait. If I really wanted to forge weld, I should work to figure that out.

Wallace's knowledge came in handy one day when I brought an old forge-welded tomahawk (with a failed weld) to my wife's cousin Chris Olin, who is an expert with tig and mig welders. In applying the welding tip to repair the old weld there was an occasional "snapping" sound like a cap gun. With each "snap," Chris would have to stop and clean the fouling off the welding tip; he even changed tips. Moreover, each "snap" would spray shiny little blobs of translucent material next to the newly welded seams *and* on the welding tips. After three or four "snaps," I tested the blobs with a file and found them to be glass-like. I showed Chris and theorized about the old recipes for flux. It seemed that Chris was reassured to know that nothing was wrong with his welding equipment or the steel. He dutifully pressed on to finish the job, "snaps" and all.

For my own part, I was glad that I could use my historical knowledge to give him some insight. Moreover, I felt a connection with history because the tomahawk in my possession had been forged in the Eighteenth century manner in which sand was a common component in the flux.

The Legacy Continues

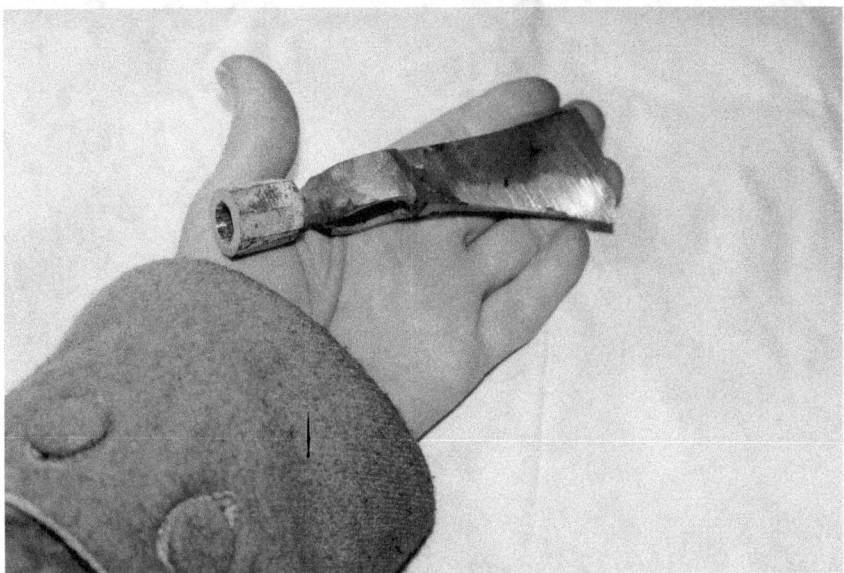

Top -In Simeon England's shop. The head, glowing orange, with bit forge welded, the eye has been punched, drifted to shape and squared with the line of the cutting edge. The constriction for pipe bowl has been started at the poll end of the head.

Bottom-The first tomahawk head, partially filed. It is a petite head, weighing well-under a pound at this stage.

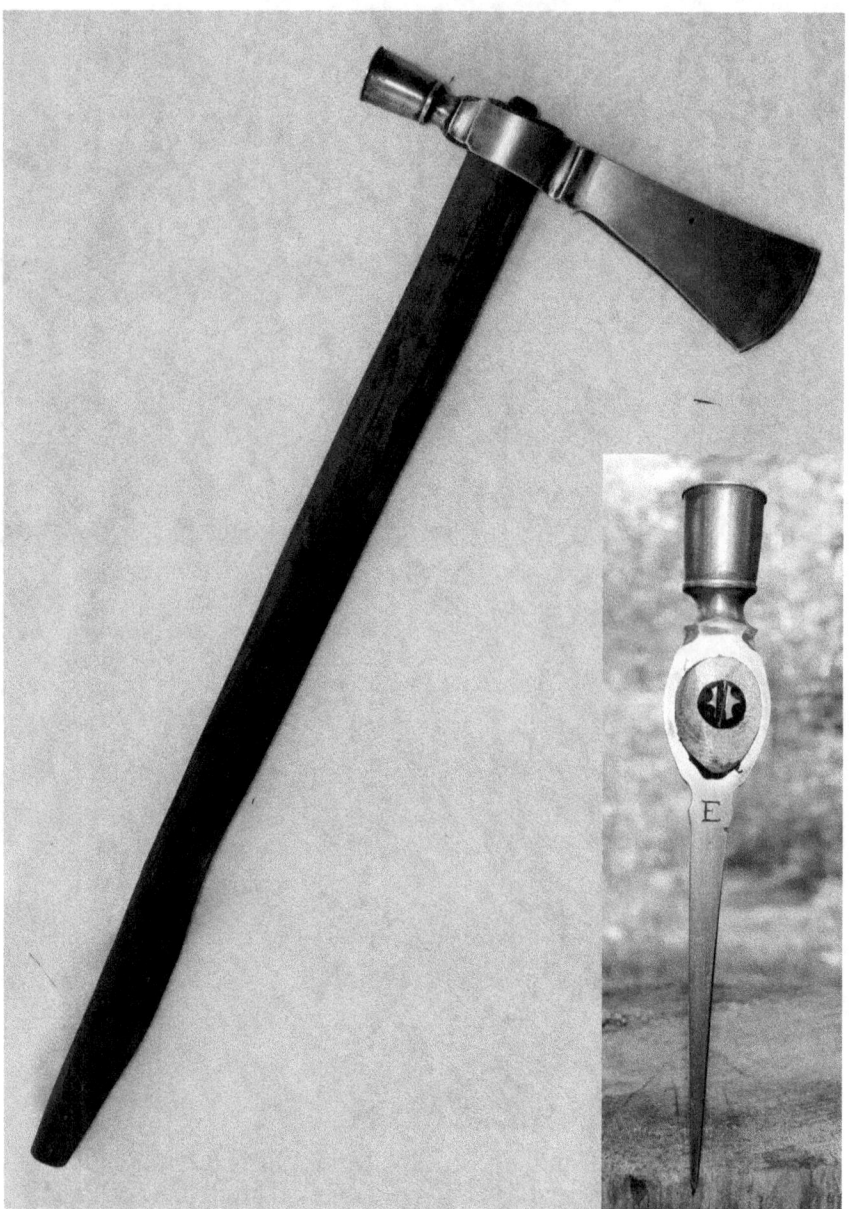

The gun-barrel tomahawk, weighing a mere 6 oz., with white ash handle eighteen inches in length and crafted with a swelled knurl. The pipe bowl is open and the handle is hot-bored for smoking. Inset-Simeon England's touch mark "E" on the top of the blade. The stopper is an engrailed iron screw.

Chapter 16
The Commodity of Skill, The Value of Experience

In conclusion, the story of Deerfoot is one which includes making not only one rifle from a kit, but one rifle prior to Deerfoot and four long-guns and several pistols over the years after Deerfoot's conversion to flint. It represents, then as now, a number of stepping stones for my experiences, all of which were, and still are, deeply rooted in the historical context of muzzleloaders.

It should also be noted that my most used rifle is a mid-18th century .58 caliber Virginia style flintlock, a style that predates the Tennessee rifle by about 50 years.

The Virginia rifle was crafted by the late Glen Jones, a Colonial Williamsburg-trained master gunsmith. It is expertly executed in the style of the James River school, sporting a Brown Bess butt-plate and the trimmed down shape of that same iconic British military musket. It has been a joy to shoot for over 25 years and is: an emblem of talents honed into a body of skills.

I probably would not have appreciated the Virginia Rifle nearly as much, if I had not first tried my hand at assembling Deerfoot and all the other muzzleloading firearms. In the simplest analysis, if I not tried something *just a little outside of my comfort zone*, like the project that converted Deerfoot to a flintlock, I would never have realized a new path of study that led me to a deep and abiding passion for living history, and especially of the eighteenth and early nineteenth centuries.

Long before I tried my hand at the flintlock kit, I had

developed my own skill set for working leather and sewing fabric as well, but those did not just appear out of the ether. Each skill set was, instead, the consequence of several desires.

    As a teenager during the mid-1970's, I searched high and low for historical "looking" items to satisfy my lust for all things hunter-trapper-mountain man. The most notable pursuit that became the seed of change, was a strong desire to buy an expensive pair of so-called moccasin boots. I made several adamant pleas which were met with my parents' equally, if not more, adamant refusals.

    Little did I know, they had recognized my knack for making a number of leather pouches, which moved them to discuss the matter between themselves for several days. A week or so later, I was asked about my willingness to try making a similar pair of boots. When I said yes, my parents put me to the test. My father and I drove to the Tandy leather store in Springfield, Virginia, where he purchased half a tanned steer hide and an "Apache-Boot pattern so that I could make my own knee-high footwear. A month later I had a finished pair of handsewn boots. Thereafter, the adults and peers who saw my finished work encouraged my efforts.

    My own path from the 20th century back into the past began right there when I focused on developing my talents into a useful skill, but even that experience is only half of the chapter.

    The second notable pursuit began during that same time, when I could not find the "historical shirt" of my desires, in the modern department stores, or craft shops or outdoor catalogs. My mother had made one for me, but one was not enough. I finally located something called a "ponderosa shirt" in a moccasin catalog. It was expensive,

The Comodity of Skill, The Value of Experience

not to mention too short in the body and the sleeves were also too short and frustratingly constricted. Still, I wore it just the same, albeit with an added set of front and back extensions so it would remain tucked in pants.

The ill-fitting nature of that commercially-made shirt was enough to convince me that if I wanted another "old style" shirt that fit comfortably, I was not going to find one in the stores or catalogs. I would have to have my mother make more. My mother complied with my request, but only after constant urging, which some might refer to as "nagging."

In two years, she had sewn five of my shirts. One shirt of note consisted of a yoke (over the shoulders) made from an old feed bag with a blue printed pattern.[27] I dearly loved that shirt, especially due to my mother's appreciation of the American farm-culture use of the feed bag during the early 20th century.

I also highly respected her talents which manifested themselves in several sewing projects (which she humbly showed me) from her teenage years as a farm girl in 4-H. I had not known about them until she removed them from an old dresser, where they had been hidden for decades. These items revealed her excellent skills as a seamstress.

Though she loved to help her sons, she had little desire to be presented with endless sewing projects. She had already coached me in the use of her Viking sewing machine, several years earlier, so that in her words she, *"would see to it that my boys could tend to their own sewing needs."* With that background, she taught me how to fit together a basic pullover shirt.

In the end, thanks to her guiding hand and determination, her thirteen-year-old son would acquire a comfort level making shirts and other clothes on her sewing machine.

    That nudge from my mother moved me to make, or attempt to make, the desired item myself. What started with boots and shirts, translated into beading hatbands, tanning furs and skins, assembling knives along with their 1800's sheaths, making archery equipment, a coon fur vest, and an assortment of other kitchy frontier stuff.

    Almost a decade later, I took my first steps into the world of the "buckskinning-rendezvous." There I encountered many home-made items on trade blankets and in the trader's tents that I figured I could make myself. After all, I had been making my own moccasins, shirts and sundry clothes long before that. I soon realized, after several camps, there was an endless variety of handmade products. It also seemed there was a collective desire, among the participants, to resurrect old skills, display and sell the products of those skills. Since I enjoyed the autonomy of making my own stuff, I felt right at home with a whole camp of "do-it-yourself'ers."

    What I did not realize at the time was that my own endeavor to resurrect old skills was, in fact, part of a huge movement, during the 1970's and into the 1980's. It was seen as a "get back to the basics" movement.

    Folks were trying to reconnect with their past by pursuing the old-fashioned matters of plain living like: making soap, tanning hides, eating wild edibles, making shoes, dressing hogs, raising heirloom plants, weaving, blacksmithing and making black powder rifles, just to name a few.

    Another growing hobby which shared similar roots and overlapped with the "plain living" movement was buckskinning, which many identify as a *way of life*. It too became fertile ground for that re-connection, especially

The Comodity of Skill, The Value of Experience

the ethic to use only tools from the pre-1840 time period to create its products.

Practitioners not only felt empowered, but they enjoyed fruits of their new-found independence. Thus, the two ethics - plain living and buckskinning - spread across the nation and beyond, which led the general public to ask, 'what was the allure in resurrecting a bunch of old-timey stuff?' The answer was summed up by author, Dick "Beau Jacques" House, in his chapter on *Why Buckskinners Create*, from Chapter One in the **Book of Buckskinning II.**[28]

"Buckskinning is the only hobby, whether followed on American soil or in distant lands, in which making your own equipment is, by the very nature of the pastime, as much a part of it as the enjoyment of the hobby itself.

There, in a nub, is the reason that buckskinners have returned to the primitive crafts and simple ways of producing not only the vintage-styled weapons they shoot, but the utensils they use, the lodges that shield them from the elements, the coverings on their backs, legs and feet, and the foofurraw and finery that lends style and dash to their outfits.

Without its arts, its crafts and its creativity, buckskinning would be without a very essential dimension. You don't' have to build your own, but your enjoyment of buckskinning is enhanced if you can...and do." [29]

Notice that Dick House avoided the words "all" and "everything" in reference to making your own stuff. I seemed to have missed that in my early years, and for a time, I tried to do it all. In theory, I could perhaps make anything that I put my mind to.

After all, buckskinners, just like their counterparts in the historical trapper, hunter, and explorer, are a multitalented and resourceful group just as those modern-day folks who are farmers, ranchers and others living in isolated pockets of the country. Resourcefulness is, in a matter of speaking, a part of the job description for working with a number of things, whether it's machinery, cooking, growing food and livestock, or fabricating tools.

Though I liked being resourceful, I finally had to admit to myself, after several years of trying, that in reality, I did not have time to make everything. I was struggling just to keep myself in clothing and footwear, so I needed to be a good deal more selective than I had been.

That being said, I still believe that an important facet of the "do-it-yourself" mind-set for me has always been, stepping out of my comfort zone just far enough to try a number of different projects; observing where I excelled and where I did not.

My own hands-on experiences have increased my appreciation of the people whose hands skillfully guided the tools which made the old antique furniture, cabinets, firearms and even the simple food-bowls. Those hand-crafted products do possess a certain warmth.

A significant catalyst for my journey into understanding historical life ways, came by way of the assembly and use of Deerfoot; and its inevitable conversion to a flintlock rifle. Though I was no gunsmith, assembling gun parts was within my comfort zone (drilling, tapping, filing, sanding). However, making a flintlock-lock from a kit which involved the added skill of hardening and tempering steel was not, but I was willing to try.

It made me more cognizant of others who excelled in their craft, because they continued to refine their skills in the greater context of historical methodologies. I, on the other

The Comodity of Skill, The Value of Experience

hand, sought out historical forms of moccasins, footwear, shirts and sundry clothes as well as the skills for hunting, fishing, gardening and gathering.

The contrast moved me to question long-held beliefs, like the folk-lore behind the term, *home-spun-America*. The more I researched and read, not to mention considered my own experiences, I began to realize that "total self-sufficiency" was not possible.

It is a myth that 250 years ago each family made *all* their own clothing, grew *all* their own food, and made *all* their own tools from what was available on the farm.

It is actually well documented that folks who spun sheep's-wool and linen (from flax) did *not* weave all their own cloth for clothing. They simply did not have time. There are many entries in personal accounts and store ledgers showing purchases and exchanges between people in the countryside and merchants in rural towns for bolts of linen, some of which were made locally, but many of which were, like the vast yardages of wool, imported in the Atlantic trade.

In terms of balance, I am not implying that the average colonial was not resourceful, rather the specialization of skill meant that one weaver, for instance, generally wove the thread spun by the women in eight or ten homes of a settlement. Weavers would therefore travel in a circuit to any number of towns to ply their trade. Specialization is after all, a manifestation of an economy based upon time, skill and experience.

I eventually saw my own efforts as a balancing act in which there were opportunities to try endless projects myself, versus efficiently using my time and plying my skills in a couple of areas that allowed me to specialize, whereby I could provide a commodity. I could then trade my commodity for that of another skilled person.

The relevance of specialization could not have been more true than when I purchased my first smith-made tomahawk, in 1989, from Keith Johnson. Though it still displays some of the forging marks, that does not detract from the fact that it is an expertly made tool with graceful lines. I view those forge marks as an echo of the rugged resilience of the piece.

I have ever since cherished the purchase, because it has been a durable product that has served me well for over three decades. Keith, at that time, was one of only a handful of master bladesmiths making tomahawks in the upper mid-west. Keith also has the distinction of forge-welding a working wrought iron rifle barrel.

I believe it is highly relevant to reference people like Mike Miller, Simeon England, Wallace Gusler and Keith Johnson, and Eugene Shadley because they are masters at their trade. It is worth my time to listen to them and learn from their example. It is worth my money to purchase products from their hands which represent, the sum of all their mistakes and corrections, their wins and losses, their break-downs and breakthroughs. In short, I am the recipient of a commodity in their skills, and the value of my purchase is their experience.

If there is any nugget to "take-away" from the Journey of Deerfoot it is: Don't be afraid to step out of your comfort zone to test your talents; to satisfy an itch to resurrect an old skill; to shoot a flintlock and ultimately (for me) pursue the nagging question of, *"Can I hunt with this rifle, like my ancestors did?"* Though I am thankful for my own persistence that pushed me to make the actual flint-lock

The Comodity of Skill, The Value of Experience

itself, it was not the end goal or the final prize for me.

The new lock was a spring board which transformed my longrifle from a caplock into a flintlock and gave me a greater sense of resourcefulness. It provided me with a vehicle to travel back to an earlier time. It allowed me to support myself by hunting with a technology akin to that of the early longhunters, eastern explorers, and newcomers to places like the Shenendoah Valley, New River and Cumberland Gap.

My goal was and remains: to see through the eyes of an early mountaineer or eastern hunter and relearn what they understood as common knowledge. The conversion that resulted in a flintlock was a means to an end that became a pallet for correcting my mistakes, overcoming my breakdowns and, in the process, deepening my insight.

In the final examination, a gun-barrel tomahawk being worked by the hands of a master is but the latest in a long line of projects that will continue to add to the legacy of my first flintlock. That humble longrifle was a welcome, early mile marker on a long, winding, sometimes frustrating and uncertain trail. The benefits of walking that trail, however, have not only added to my appreciation of the eighteenth century, but, especially, provided me with personal fulfillment from nearly four decades of using flintlocks that began in the simplest of manners, as:

          My journey with Deerfoot.

Top-Author with Wallace Gusler at Martin's Station, Ewing VA, May 2006.
Bottom - Author with Simeon England at his forge in Edmonton KY, March 2022.

Chapter 17
The Tennessee Rifle

A Brief Chronicle of Style and Utility
With Comments from Master Gunsmith, Mike Miller

In the early years of our new nation, families from the western regions of Virginia and North Carolina emigrated into East Tennessee and Cumberland River basin, bringing with them a number of family traditions.

One such tradition was the art of gun-making as a "family trade," emerging from the roots of the gun-making schools of South West Virginia and North Carolina. The architectural lines of what we now in the Twenty-first century, identify as the "Tennessee rifle" are lean and devoid of embellishment. Though the intricate carving and stylish forms of engraving found on the earlier pieces commonly made during the colonial era were well known to these gun makers, the average customer was motivated by the need for a more utilitarian gun.

The "Tennessee style" did not happen all at once, but rather it developed over time as successor gunsmiths assumed the role of local gun makers while following behind the advancing frontier, thus tending to the needs of settlers who were otherwise several week's ride from the gunsmiths of the east.

It is believed that the earliest guns made in the Tennessee region still utilized brass patch-boxes, nose cones and butt-plates as well as small vignettes of metal engraving on lock edges and patch box finials, but it is difficult to prove (though not impossible) due to the lack of business and census records. Of the rifles that can be linked to known Tennessee gun makers, however, it is clear that the stocks they fashioned were made quite plainly, but continued to exhibit vestiges of earlier architecture like fatter butt-stocks with wider, straighter butt plates.

As successive gun-makers moved west, their skills matured into several slightly different stylistic expressions. They birthed a new form of long gun wherein the butt-stock became decidedly slimmer, and the common iron butt plate was fashioned in a distinctly deeper crescent shape.

Even though the common forms of embellishments were abandoned for a plainer look that spoke to the utilitarian use, the artistry, was instead, expressed in the forging of iron furniture, such as the trigger guard, that still utilized gentle curves, including "C" and "S" scroll-shapes.

In my discussions with Kentucky native and noted gunsmith Mike Miller, his examination of these old guns revealed that the makers were not unsophisticated; indeed, the gunsmiths were quite competent and there are a large number of extant examples of guns made in Tennessee that evidence expert craftsmanship in the forging of iron furniture, tight wood-to-metal fit and execution of intricate mechanisms such as double-set and single-set triggers.

The customers, however, were themselves plain folks who simply needed a gun at a cheaper price and thus, no embellishment. In some cases, a "less expensive rifle" meant one made without the most basic of furniture, such as a butt-plate and a nose cap.

As an iconic piece of the back country culture, the Tennessee rifle filled a functional need for sustenance through hunting, and defense of hearth and home, kith and kin. These firearms were tools which occupied the home in an "every-day" sense so much so that even when the rifle was out of sight, each person of the household knew in an instant, where to find it when it was needed.

Wives who stayed at home to care for the children and keep the home fires burning, could load and wield the long arms for defense or other needs such as keeping pesky varmints out of the garden.

From an early age, children of both sexes were taught the proficient use of the longrifle for hunting as well as protection of the homestead. Young boys were encouraged to carry, handle and shoot these rifles with confidence and efficiency. These children were not born with the rifle in their hands, but to an outsider it might seem so.

Regions and Makers

Anyone new to the study of these early Tennessee makers needs to understand that the oldest tradition of gunmaking is in East Tennessee, due to the migration of settlers, mainly from Virginia and North Carolina who followed well known roads, trails and rivers into the region. Though the stylistic expressions of the iron work in East Tennessee differ from that of Middle Tennessee, the common theme seems to be the architecture of the gun-stocks that have similar lines and continued use of a moderately profiled cheek piece. Moreover, East Tennessee (which has several variations from north to south) and that of Middle Tennessee, are both earlier and different than those of West Tennessee.

Today, scholars have put certain styles into what are called "schools" of makers based upon names of the gunsmiths and/or regions of geography. The schools in turn are differentiated by the shape of the stock, butt-plate, fore-end, lock plate, trigger guard and patch box, (if any), and to whom subtle stylistic variations may be attributed. The attributes within the schools also reference the dimensions of the barrel as well as the use of iron and brass.

In my discussions with Mike Miller, one of his first comments was, "Historical makers simply made rifles. Though they made them in their own style, they were still just rifles."

The East Tennessee Region

The common trait found on guns of this region is the nearly over-all use of iron mountings – butt plate, trigger guard, ramrod pipes, entry-pipe, side plate, toe plate, and nose-cap. There was also the manifestation of longer tangs on the breech plugs, as well as the development of elongated patch-boxes referred to as "banana boxes." Though a few were brass, most of them, (especially later ones) were forged from iron.

An early maker of rifles in East Tennessee, with strong connections to Virginia is Joseph Bogle, (b-July 5, 1759 York, PA; d-April 1, 1811 Blount, TN), who lived and worked in Blount County in East Tennessee. He came from a family of weavers. Though sources are unsure where his training came from, his method of carving and overall architecture of rifles is strongly associated with the Valley of Virginia, namely Augusta County, where Joseph's father received a patent for land in the southern portion of the county (now Rockbridge County). Bogle saw service in the Revolutionary War and was present for the fighting at Yorktown, Virginia. Some of the measurements of a rifle made by Bogle are as follows:

Length (overall) 61"; the barrel is octagonal (straight not swamped) and measures 44 ½", and the bore is .46 caliber. The barrel is secured to the stock by four iron keys (instead of pins) that pass through four iron thimbles. The

The Tennessee Rifle

keys are supported by iron escutcheons (as opposed to no escutcheons on earlier pieces) on both sides of the stock. The tang at the breech is approximately 3" with a single screw through to and threaded into the trigger plate (later tangs are 5-1/2 to 6-3/4" long).The lock is marked "Ketland & Co" and measures 4 ¾ long by 1" tall; which is secured by two lock bolts through iron side washers. It has double-set triggers, and an iron trigger guard. The iron patchbox is two piece and sports a spade-shaped finial; the release is in the center of the butt-plate. The length of the pull is 13-¾". The butt plate is 1-11/16" wide and 4-9/16" comb to toe (later butt plates are often thinner at 1-1/4" wide and shorter at 4-1/4 to 4-3/8"comb to toe).

One of Mike's most often cited references is the well-known maker, Elisha Bull, (b. 1791- d. 1873), who made guns for poor mountain folks; what some may analogously refer to as "the 870 Express [Remington] of its day." The Tennessee rifles often had what Mike termed as "dead-plain" maple stocks which were softer than the harder curly maple stocks. There is no real difference in choice between the plain and curly maple as the makers and customers had both available for their use. He also pointed out in his conversations with another noted master gunsmith and Virginia native, Wallace Gusler, that the people of that time and place, "had the best [wood] available and could choose the wood that they wanted to use for a gun stock." It should also be pointed out that the "utilitarian" guns which did not possess any butt plate or nose cap were in turn lower in cost, but did not lack workmanship, and were just as useful.

Mike also mentioned that, though plain and curly maple stocks are quite common for Tennessee rifles, they were not, however, the ubiquitous wooden vehicles for these rifles.

He has seen and handled guns which were also stocked in walnut ranging from light color tones to those darkened to an almost plumb black. There are a number of examples extant of cherry with deep, red hues and the occasional "mineral" streak imbedded in the grain of the wood. The stocks, true to form, are noticeably devoid of carving. The simple lines are graceful and pleasing.

Regardless of the wood though, Mike assured me, "These rifles remained utilitarian pieces and most had the dents and scratches to prove it."

Another rifle maker associated with Tennessee is Elisha Bull's brother John Valentin Bull, (b 14 February, 1777 Hartford, MD -d 21 October, 1840 Bear Creek, Marion Alabama). He was married to Fetnah (Bean) Bull, 3 April 1806 in Grainger County, Tennessee. John worked with his in-laws, the Beans, who were a rather well-known family of gun makers from Upper Tennessee.

Gunsmith William Bean had explored with Daniel Boone in the 1780's, and is said to be the first white man to establish a permanent home, and Bean's Station, west of the Allegheny Mountains. Many of his descendants became gunsmiths and are most associated (by arms collectors) with the East Tennessee School of gun-making. Many Tennessee rifles in general, have characteristics which can be attributed to the Beans.

One iconic characteristic, on some rifles for instance, is use of a thin strip of iron applied to the stock from the tang of the breech plug, reaching to the comb of the butt-plate.

As alluded to earlier, references to Tennessee rifles being "well-used" often appear in a fashion similar to this description of the "Rice Duncan" rifle which was the subject of an Essay: Rice Duncan's Longrifle: A Study of the East Tennessee Longrifle Tradition, by Jessi White; [30]

"[T]he Rice Duncan rifle is a classic example of the Tennessee longrifle profile. Close examination of the rifle reveals copious amounts of scratches, scuffs, and dents as well as a missing screw on the gun butt; this, coupled with the restrained design features helps to reinforce the idea that the gun was used mainly as a utilitarian piece rather than a show piece." [31]

By way of reference, the inspiration for Deerfoot was the heavily curled J.G. Gross rifle as shown in the book The Kentucky Rifle by Merrill Lindsay.[32]

The parts, however, which came with the kit for Deerfoot, I later identified with other makers. Though some of the parts share characteristics with Gross, My sense now is that they are more strongly associated with Baxter Bean, such as: the lobate termination of the toe-plate; the rounded extensions (feet) of the trigger guard, the rounded stock of the grip rail on the trigger guard, and the tang of the breech-plug that extends nearly to the comb of the stock.

If Deerfoot would have been made in the 1810 to 1825 time period, I do not believe it would have utilized a Germanic lock with a pointed tail, but rather a Ketland flintlock with a pinched-tail lock plate, or a rounded tail similar to a Manton.

The Middle Tennessee Region

During my conversations with Mike, he suggested that I might want to peruse some photos and a description by Mel Hankala, of a rifle made by John Wilson of Tennessee. Mel is the author of the book, **Into the Bluegrass: Art and Artistry of Kentucky's Historic Icons**, and the owner of American Historic Services, LLC, in Hitchens KY.

Mel has studied longrifles of Appalachia and the Highland Rim (Virginia, North Carolina, Kentucky and Tennessee) for a number of decades. He possesses a depth of knowledge about these firearms that few can claim.

After viewing the photos, I had a chance to confer with Mel, who reiterated what he had written and posted online about this Middle Tennessee rifle (and its maker), namely, that he had,

"Picked up a pretty cool iron mounted antique today. 46 inch - .52 caliber barrel signed: Jno. Wilson. Wilson came to Tennessee about the same time as Thomas Simpson, William Young, and Gasper Mansker. He was one of the signers of the Cumberland Compact in 1780. He later moved eastward (circa 1825) to Craig's Creek, Boutetourt County, Virginia." [33]

One of my first questions was to inquire about the time period. Mel cautiously stated that it was probably 1800 to 1805 given the use of a Ketland Lock. The rifle's patch box, butt plate, toe plate and trigger guard were of iron. The breech-plug tang was about four inches long, the pointed finial of which essentially echoed the mortises for the lock and side plate. The noticeably wider butt plate spoke to the styles of earlier guns of Virginia or Pennsylvania with a gentle curve, unlike the radical curve of the post 1815 era. The gun's maker is identified by the name engraved in a silver inset of the barrel: "Jno Wilson" in cursive form set against a stylish outline.

Even though there are bits of embellishment on this rifle it remains a utilitarian "work-horse." Though it is a heavier gun, it is not clunky. It is rather graceful with clean lines, bereft of carving which remains the common denominator among Tennessee rifles in general. The stock is black in appearance, but in the wear spots the observer can easily see that it is stocked in curly maple. From my discussions with Mel, and in looking at the photographs of the rifle, it is clear that even early-on, at the turn of the century, the stocks were being made with no embellishment.

Other notable eighteenth century makers, of the Middle Tennessee region, worth researching are: Samuel Crockett and Charles Snyder.

What's in a Name?

A number of scholars and modern rifle makers use the term Tennessee rifle, to reference not just the same basic East Tennessee design, but also styles of rifles that were literally made in the Tennessee region. As for the other contemporary monikers: Mountain Rifle, Iron Mounted Southern Rifle, and Heavy Iron-mounted Southern Rifle, tend to be used in marketing the rifles and kits for rifles, but are nonetheless still apt descriptions of the actual weight (eight to ten pounds) and solid nature of the rifles made with iron mountings. (My own rifle, named Ultimus, is just such a rifle; being 9-3/8 pounds, with a straight barrel, 42" in length and 15/16 across the flats. It is bored in .54 caliber with a flintlock ignition, and of course a very plain maple stock).

Another subject worthy of research is the use of "bloomeries" in Tennessee. These are iron furnaces scattered throughout the several regions, that refined and made iron for use in gun barrels, the iron furniture or mountings on the stocks, as well as iron bars. This is perhaps one of the reasons for the early and continued use of iron (instead of brass) on most Tennessee rifles; there are however, no absolutes.

As alluded to by several of the "marketing titles," these guns generally featured a heavier straight octagon barrel (as opposed to a swamped barrel with a waist about two-thirds up from the breech toward the muzzle) which was often rifled, but could also have a smooth bore. Another feature included the use of double set triggers which allowed the shooter to use the back trigger to set the front trigger to a lighter pull or "hair-trigger." This was done to avoid "trigger creep" and thus improve accuracy.

Perhaps the "fanciest" attribute found on some Tennessee rifles is the use of curly maple that often displays a pleasing "tiger-striped" pattern or "curly" grain which naturally created its own decoration, God's handiwork, if you will. Due to the pleasing grain structure commonly found in maple wood, though not always, the curly-maple stocks did not beg for any enhancement, such as additional carving. The beauty of the wood was drawn out by the use of aqua fortis applied to the stock, then heated with a hot iron held close to the surface of the wood, which would react with the nitric acid to darken the wood. With the application of linseed oil, the curl in the wood was deepened and enhanced, creating a contrast between light and dark stripes.

By 1820, census records reveal the presence of at least 38 makers and 68 employees in Tennessee. Out of those numbers, East Tennessee could boast 25 (or 66%) of these businesses. In Middle Tennessee there were 13 operations that were also doing well with a proportionate share of the business. By 1830 the biggest change would be the installation and use of caplocks. The more urban gunsmiths would, by and large, embrace this change, whereas the more isolated pockets of makers and shooters would resist it and continue to use the flintlock ignition.[34] Whatever the ignition system,

The Tennessee Rifle

the Tennessee rifle had filled a need and would endure in its popularity for decades to come from Tennessee to Texas and beyond.

In the present day it can commonly be found at black powder venues, historical gatherings and hunting camps where it continues, in its "restrained demeanor," to be quite useful and durable.

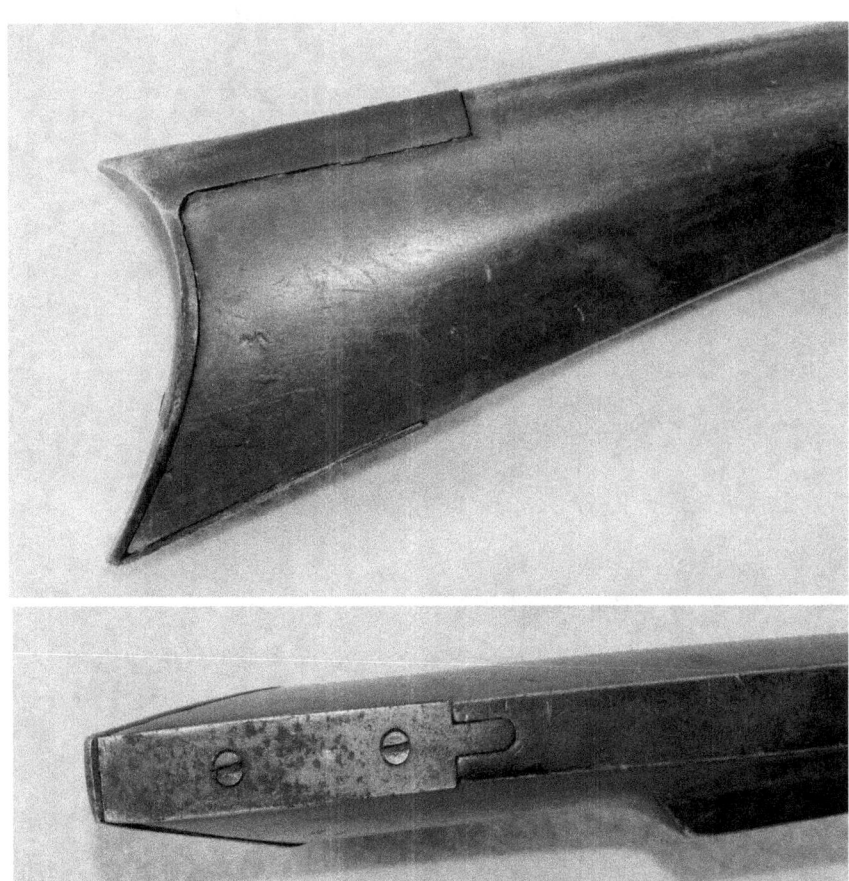

Photos of Deerfoot, and its resemblence to Bean architecture:
Top-Deeply curved butt plate with elongated comb.
Bottom-Toe plate showing finial extension with lobate terminus.

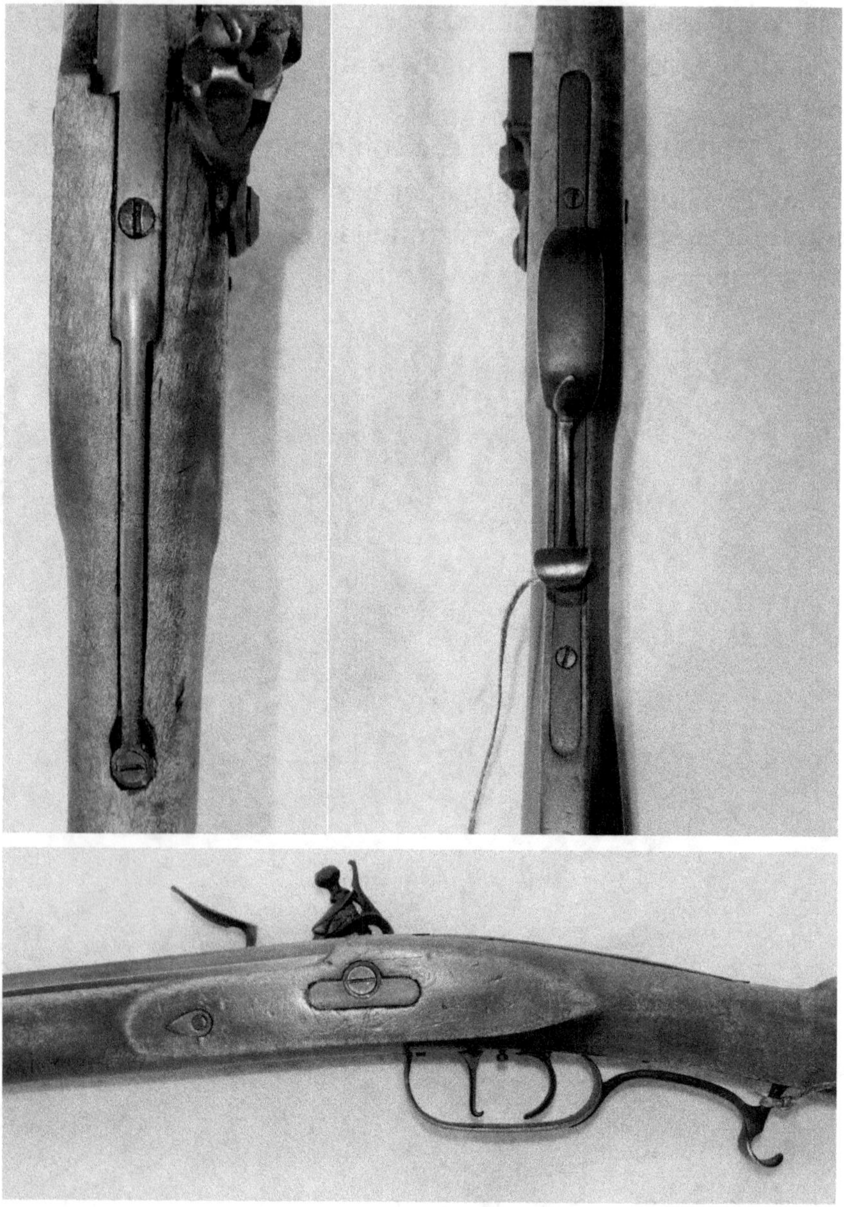

My Journey with Deerfoot

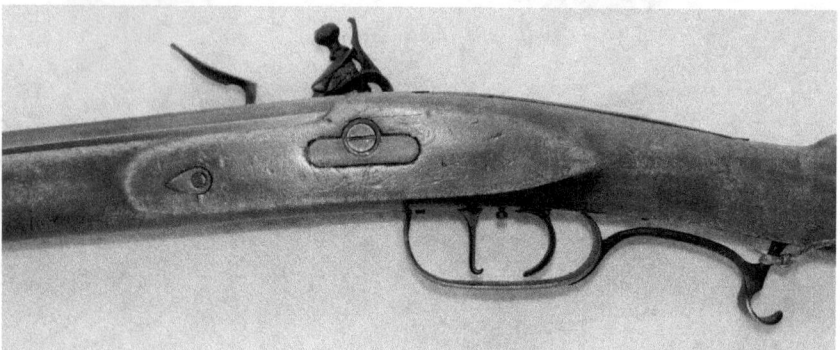

Photos of Deerfoot and it's resemblance to Bean architecture:
Top left-the long "popcicle" tang inlet into the top of the wrist.
Top right-Trigger guard with rounded grip rail and long lobular feet
Bottom-Bean side plate (for lock), trigger guard showing rounded grip rail terminating with open rear scroll, also double-set triggers,

End Notes

1. **The Story of Daniel Boone**, By William O. Steele, Illustrated by Warren Baumgarten, copyright 1953, Young Readers Press, New York, a subsidiary of Ace Publishing, Published by arrangement with Grosset and Dunlap Inc. first printing, 1969.

***Book Author's note** – William O. Steele was a resident of Franklin Tennessee who loved sharing the lore of the area with children. He often spoke to the mountaineers whose families had been in the area for generations. He also spoke with members of the local Cherokee people. He felt these two groups were our strongest link to the past.

2. A **capote** (ka-POE) is a long coat generally made from heavy wool like a trade blanket or duffel.

3. A "**cleaning jag**" is a cylindrical, barbed end-attachment, slightly smaller than the inside diameter of the barrel. It is screwed onto a ramrod to wipe the inside of the bore. A small piece of cloth envelopes the end of the jag, which is then worked up and down the barrel. The jag also helps center the end of the ramrod touching the round ball or other projectile.

4. The **F designation of black powder**, The term Fg is a designation for the size of black powder grains. It is derived from a screen with 24 wires per inch (12 warp, 12 woof) that is used to separate and grade dry black powder. "F" stands for "fine" and "g" stands for "grain." The screen allows smaller granules to pass, but retains the larger ones. The designations for black powder are:

Fg (one F) is generally used for small canon but also large bore guns like .80 and .90 caliber. 24 per inch (12 x 12),

FFg (two F or double F) gernerally, is considered rifle powder for .54 caliber and larger as well as powder for larger long-guns and fowling pieces. 32 wires per inch (16 x16), FFFg (three F or triple F) is used for pistols and smaller bore rifles, .45 caliber and smaller. 40 wires per inch (20 x 20), FFFFg (four F) is used for priming a flintlock. 80 wires per inch (40 x 40).

When loading, the powder is measured by *volume* of grains.

5. **Rabbits,** in this instance, refers to varying hares also called "snowshoe" hares in the mid-west.

6. Reginald Laubin and Gladys Laubin, ***The Indian Tipi, Its History Construction and Use.*** (University of Oklahoma Press, 1957), (First Ballantine Books Edition: August 1971, sixth printing 1981).

7. Bernard DeVoto, **Across the Wide Missouri**, Houghton Mifflin Company, Boston, 1947.

8. **Rain pegs** are short two to three inch sticks approximately one quarter inch in diameter which are placed on the underside of each tipi pole and held in place by the liner rope. Rain water can be channeled down the underside of the pole using capillary tension and directed between the two rain pegs, it will then continue down the pole to the ground. The purpose is to prevent precipitation moisture from dripping into the tipi randomly from all the poles and direct it to the ground.

9. A **drum bolster** is a cylinder that screws into the side of the breech end of the barrel, right where a touch hole should be. Drum bolsters enabled the shooters of the 19th century to convert their flintlocks to caplocks by drilling out the touch hole, threading the bored hole, screwing in the small drum and then drilling a hole near the top of the drum to fit a nipple pointed at the front of the cock, for ignition with a caplock.

10. **10-40 thread** – This is not a very common thread.

End Notes

It is generally found in pre-1980 sewing machines, small mechanical devices and gun parts.

11. **Clatch** is a word that mimics the sound of the lock snapping against the frizzen with no spark, no flash.

12. **Hang-fire** is a term which describes the "hang" time (delay) from the flash of the powder in the pan until the ignition of the powder inside the barrel of a flintlock ignition. (In a caplock, it refers to the delay from the time the cock has struck and ignited the cap until ignition in the barrel.) IF the touch hole is properly placed, repeated hang-fire ignitions in a short string generally mean a dirty powder or poor powder. Also, the barrel may need to be swabbed, and the flash pan should be wiped out.

13. A **flash-in-the-pan** is the occurrence of the powder in the pan flashing, but the charge in the barrel does not ignite, hence, the gun does not fire. This occurrence often means the touch-hole is blocked and needs to be cleared. Repeated ocurrences could mean that the projectile has been loaded without powder, otherwise known as a "dry ball."

14. The **lock cover** A sewn piece of tanned skin, oiled leather or contoured piece of rawhide which is tied to and covers the lock area of a flintlock firearm, which, in essence, provides a tiny roof over the lock area to protect it from precipitation and snow hanging from branches. See images for pattern and form pages 67-68 supra.

Also, it has been referred to by some as "cow's knee," but the Author believes that the term is from some time after the middle of the 19th century, in reference to the bulge of a "cow's knee" Author has not found the term in 18th century writings. However; the term "lock cover" has been found in a number of 18th century writings.

15. **Baker, Mark A. 1986. "A Pilgrim's Journey: Trekking Tips,"** *Muzzleloader Magazine,* Scurlock Publishing, Texarkana TX , September/October 1986, 13. Subsequently published in: *Muzzleloader Magazine's* A Pilgrim's Journey Volume One 1986-1995, Chapter One 1986 September/October, *Trekking Tips,* p. 9.

16. **In the White** a term referencing a completed gun which does not have finished wood, or metal parts. Some metal parts, whether iron or brass, may need to be further sanded and polished before being considered "finished. The wood generally requires light emory cloth, steel wool or historically scraping before it is ready for a treatment such as aqua fortis followed by linseed oil. (it is often prudent to neutralize the nitric acid with soda water and dry it before applying the linseed oil.

17. **Aqua fortis (meaning strong water)**
Aqua fortis, also known as *nitrate of iron*, is a corrosive solution made with water, nitric acid, and iron. Commercial nitric acid is 68% grade. The most basic formula for aqua fortis is; 4 parts water to which is added one part nitric acid, followed by small pieces of iron or mild steel (i.e. 1005). This should be done in a well ventilated area as it will create vapors (red in color) that are caustic and cause choking.

Nitric acid in its purest form will "passivize" or create a coating and react very little with other mediums like metallic objects, therefore water is added to overcome this occurrence, and thus make it more reactive. Due to the added water, the 68% is considered an "azeotrope" and expressed as; HNO_3.

18. **Barrel springing** is also known as "harmonic vibration" in the barrel which is, after all, a hollow tube. A soft rest will absorb the vibration and the barrel is unaffected by the shock

of ignition that causes vibration. A hard rest, on the other hand, will resist the vibration caused by the shock of ignition, resulting in the vibration being cast, like a whip, back up into the barrel, away from the hard rest. The result is the muzzle being cast upwardly and away from the point of aim.

19. **Pulling the wad** from over-the-shot with a tow worm, and replacing the shot with a round ball. **A Toast to the Fur Trade**, *A Picture Essay on Its Material Culture*, by Robert C. Wheeler, Illustrations by David Christofferson, Edited by Ardis Hillman Wheeler, Wheeler Productions, publisher, copyright 1985, page 69, references-

"*Figure* 3 Gun worm excavated at the 1802-1803 Yellow River post in Wisconsin. Gun worms were necessary to remove or unload a charged musket. There were often times when the hunter, with musket loaded with shot, came upon a large animal like a moose, deer or bear, and it was necessary to change to a ball." and

"Letter 72 from James Isham at York Fort, 20 July, 1739, stated defects in certain trade goods as reported by Indians: *"Gunworms is very unhandy, being short and too wide for a ramrod, they being obliged to put a piece of paper round the ramrod before the worm will be fast, by which reason they lose many a deer etc. before they have time to draw the small shot to put a ball in."* [Letters from Hudson Bay, 1703-40, page 279.]

20. A **vent pick** is a probe with a point as fine as a needle, used to clear out the touch hole or vent on the side of the barrel utilizing a flintlock ignition.

21. **Patching** is cloth and, in some cases, thin hide, used by wrapping around the round ball and then pushing the round ball into the barrel creating a friction fit. The patch holds the round ball in place against the powder and engages the

rifling as it in turn grips the round ball.

22. A **turn-screw** is an old name for a screw driver. It is often forged with a loop for a handle, permitting the user to apply greater torque.

23. A **range rod** is a loading rod often made of brass or aluminum, with a handle or knob at one end and a jag of a certain caliber at the other and almost always fitted with a barrel-saver, often called a do-nut or muzzle protector. This is used to load the gun while shooting at a range or other place when not on the hunt. It is often the first resort for cleaning the gun.

24. A **trail walk,** also known as a "woods walk" is a competition event often seen at muzzleloading camps, in which teams consisting of several people follow a scenario determined by the era and geography and even historical persons. Targets are presented for shooting or opting not to shoot, along with other skills with tomahawk, knife and perhaps timed fire-starting as well. There is usually identification of historical objects, along with plants and animals (animal parts). It is also common to pose questions on history.

25. **Loops and pins** are the most common way in which longrifles with full stocks are attached to the barrels. The loops are actually "T" shaped pieces of steel or soft metal, with a hole drilled to accept the pin. The top of the "T" fits (upside-down) into the dovetail on the barrel with the trunk of the "T" (pointing away from the barrel) being the place where the hole is drilled for the pin.

26. The DVD - **Making a Handforged Tomahawk, with Wallace Gusler**, copyright 2018 American Pioneer Video-Historical Enterprises LLC, Galatin, TN.

27. The feed stores sold feed in cloth bags in an array of

fabric prints which would be used by the farm wives to make clothes for the children. Generally buying two bags of the same print-pattern, lent enough fabric for the project to produce a dress or shirt.

28. House, Dick "Beau Jacques," 1983, *Why Buckskinners Create*, in **Book of Buckskinning II**, 1-12, Texarkana TX., Rebel Publishing Company.

29. Id at p.2.

30. **Rice Duncan's Longrifle**: *A Study of the East Tennessee Longrifle Tradition*, by Jessi White, Journal of Backcountry Studies, Vol 8, Number 1 (Spring 2014). Available on line at http:/libjournal.uncg.edu/jbc/article/download/923/578.

31 Id at p.3.

32. **The Kentucky Rifle**, by Merrill Lindsay, photography by Bruce Pendleton, Arma Press & the Historical Society of York County (1972).

33. Phone conversation with **Mel Hankala,** 23 February, 2022, following his on-line posting of the photos and comments on John Wilson's early Tennessee rifle.

34. **A Preliminary Survey of Historic Period Gunmaking in Tennessee**, by Samuel D. Smith, Fred M. Prouty, and Benjamin C. Nance, 1991, Tennessee Dept of Conservation, Division of Archaeology Report of Investigations No. 8. Public Document Authorization No. 327343. References taken from Pages 23 - 29.

My Journey with Deerfoot

Author's Biography

John and Connie (his wife of twenty-eight years) live in the hills of northern Minnesota near the town of Cohasset. John built their colonial style house where they raised their three children (now adults) Sarah, Johannah, and John.

Hayes attended Bemidji State University (1980-1984) where he obtained a Bachelor of Science, majoring in both Political Science and Indian Studies, as well as Minors in Ojibwe language and Anthropology. He received his Juris Doctorate from Hamline University School of Law in 1989 and has practiced law in Itasca County, since 1991.

The author's love of history began as a four-year-old transplant to Fairfax County, Virginia where, for fifteen years, he encountered early American history and the forging of our early government. Hayes took numerous trips to George Washington's old haunts, the plantations of Mount Vernon and Woodlawn, and Jefferson's home Monticello. In addition, there were several trips to Jamestown, Colonial Williamsburg and Yorktown wherein he encountered and was intrigued by the daily lifestyles and struggles of the common person; whether those struggles came from keeping of hearth and home, sociopolitical tensions, legal endeavors, or war-time duties.

As a youth, he hunted, fished and trapped within the woods and along the waters of the piedmont and mountains of Virginia. His adventures took him from the northern border on the Potomac, to the dense woods of Albemarle and Spotsylvania Counties; and from the shores of the Chesapeake to the mountains west of the Shenendoah Valley.

Hayes has been a participant in primitive historical treks for several decades. One such trip on foot (in mocassins) the author covered thirty-three miles in three days, while carying his .58 cal fowling piece and twenty pounds of gear in his over-the-shoulder, 18th century, knapsack/haversack. He hunted for his sustenance along the way.

In addition to spending a summer on the Seagull River as a camp counselor (in 1985) in the Boundary Waters Canoe Area Wilderness (Minnesota and Ontario), Hayes has engaged in dozens of canoe trips on numerous Minnesota lakes and rivers.

In October 2014, Mark Sage, Eugene Shadley, and the author paddled, in two birchbark canoes, from upper Prairie River into the Mississippi River. The trio hunted and fished for their sustenance during the seven day endeavor.*

Hayes has also spent extended time in the saddle on primitive outings, most notably, The Boone Trace Project **, lead by Mark Sage, which lasted for the whole month of May in 2016. The Core riders of the project actually crossed the Cumberland Gap (from Virginia to Kentucky) on horseback with flintlocks and in primitive eighteenth century fashion. The Core riders were able to ride on actual parts of the Boone trace and Wilderness Road from Sycamore Shoals, TN to Boonesborough, KY.

From his Minnesota home, Hayes taps maple trees for syrup and picks wild rice in nearby lakes and rivers. He also finds satisfaction in emulating our colonial predecessors by: hunting small and large game, water fowl, and upland birds with flintlocks, as well as growing heirloom plants, practicing eighteenth century lifeways, and writing about them in magazines such as Muzzleloader and Muzzle Blasts.

Hayes maintains a web site: Huntingthroughhistory.com, where he posts his blog, presents videos he has

Author's Biography

produced, and advertises his books for sale.

*This trip was featured in three installments in **Muzzleloader Magazine,** Vol XLII, No's. 1, 2, and 3 (March/April through July/August), authored by Mark Sage.

This trip was featured in four installments in **Muzzleloader Magazine, Vol, XLIII, Nos. 4, 5, 6, and Vol XLIV No. 1 (Sept/Oct 2016 through March/April 2017), authored by Mark Sage.

www.ingramcontent.com/pod-product-compliance
Lightning Source LLC
Chambersburg PA
CBHW071911290426
44110CB00013B/1348